Overcoming Overwork

Women *at* Work
Inspiring conversations, advancing together

The **HBR WOMEN AT WORK SERIES** spotlights the real challenges and opportunities women experience throughout their careers. With interviews from the popular podcast of the same name and related articles, stories, and research, these books provide inspiration and advice for taking on topics at work like inequity, advancement, and building community. Featuring detailed discussion guides, this series will help you spark important conversations about where we're at and how to move forward.

Books in the series include:

Making Real Connections

Next-Level Negotiating

Overcoming Ageism

Overcoming Overwork

Speak Up, Speak Out

Taking Charge of Your Career

Thriving in a Male-Dominated Workplace

You, the Leader

Women *at* Work

Inspiring conversations, advancing together

Overcoming Overwork

Harvard Business Review Press
Boston, Massachusetts

The web addresses referenced in this book were live and correct at the time of the book's publication but may be subject to change.

Library of Congress Cataloging-in-Publication Data

Names: Harvard Business Review Press, issuing body.
Title: Overcoming overwork / Harvard Business Review.
Description: Boston, Massachusetts : Harvard Business Review Press, [2024]
| Series: HBR women at work series | Includes index.
Identifiers: LCCN 2024010082 (print) | LCCN 2024010083 (ebook)
| ISBN 9781647826994 (paperback) | ISBN 9781647827007 (epub)
Subjects: LCSH: Women—Employment. | Hours of labor. | Burn out
(Psychology)—Prevention. | Women—Health.
Classification: LCC HD6053 .O84 2024 (print) | LCC HD6053
(ebook) | DDC 331.4—dc23/eng/20240304
LC record available at https://lccn.loc.gov/2024010082
LC ebook record available at https://lccn.loc.gov/2024010083

ISBN: 978-1-64782-699-4
eISBN: 978-1-64782-700-7

CONTENTS

SECTION FOUR

Carve Out Time for Yourself

Contents

Protect Yourself from Overwork

by Amy Gallo, cohost of *Women at Work*

I have a confession: I hate the phrase "work-life balance."

Don't get me wrong. Maintaining a harmonious relationship between my work and my personal life sounds lovely and is definitely something worth aspiring to. But I'm just not sure how achievable it is.

When I consider the various aspects of my life, I don't see "personal" and "professional" on opposite sides of a seesaw that I'm attempting to balance effortlessly.

No. I picture a deck of cards that someone tossed in the air and let fall in a chaotic mess (52-card pickup, anyone?). The cards are the various pieces of my life, and each day I decide which to pick up and attend to and which ones to leave in the pile.

While this may sound negative, I swear it's not. It's a visual that works better for me because of the many things that my life involves. Like a lot of people, I don't just have a job and a life outside of work. I wear many hats. I cohost a podcast, deliver keynotes and workshops based on my books, write articles for HBR, star in HBR videos, and write a biweekly newsletter. And those are just some of my professional endeavors! I'm also a mom, wife, daughter, friend, and community member.

It's a full life—one I'm grateful for. But just because I chose, and enjoy, all of these roles doesn't mean that I'm immune to exhaustion and stress. In fact, everyone I know feels this way at times.

Fortunately, I recognize this isn't a "me" problem. While it's tempting to blame myself for an inability to say no or make good choices about how to spend my time, that's not what's at the root of the issue. The core problem is that I work and live in a culture of burnout and overwork. One where a perfectly normal—and frequent—response to "How are you?" is "Busy."

When that's the norm, you're going to feel strained, even if you're exceptionally good at time management, tackling your to-do list, or ruthlessly prioritizing projects. If society and organizations have unrealistic expectations for what a reasonable workday looks like and how much we can get done in our limited time, it's no wonder so many of us are burned out.

This is especially true for women, who are often expected to fill many roles, not just outside work but within it as well. Women are more likely to be given busy work, or even dead-end projects (see chapter 10 for more on that). We tend to carry an outsized burden when it comes to childcare and eldercare in comparison with our male counterparts. Many working women do what's been referred to as a "second shift," where they essentially complete another full workday after they get home from the office or close their laptop for the day.

This makes it that much more important that we find ways to protect ourselves from the negative effects of working too much by setting boundaries and reducing stress—even when that feels impossible.

That's what this book does—and I'm guessing is why you've turned to it. Perhaps like me, you'd like to know how to resist society's insistence that we are booked solid every day, give so much of ourselves to work and to other demands, and are left without time or energy for personal endeavors.

I'm not a big believer in New Year's resolutions, but I will often write down some intentions for the coming year in December or January. For the past several years, on the top of my list has been "more time for myself." Making that happen isn't easy, but it's critical. There *are* healthy ways to cope with overwork, pressure, and stress, which you'll read about in this book. They require that we do things like ask for help, delegate, prioritize mental health and self-care—and that we don't feel guilty doing so.

Section 1 lays out the problem of overwork, where it stems from, and how it affects women in particular. The blame is too often placed on the worker, but the authors in this section make the clear and cogent argument that it's not our fault. My hope is that this section will help you move away from any guilt to understand the true root causes of overwork.

The subsequent three sections include articles and podcast interview transcripts with lots of tips and advice on how to protect yourself against the negative consequences of working too much. The advice in these sections ranges from helping you identify and overcome burnout by taking breaks, controlling your schedule, delegating tasks, asking for help, and being mindful of your mental and physical health.

One of my favorite articles in this collection is the final one: "How Organizations Can Support Women's Mental Health at Work," by Kelly Greenwood. As I mentioned earlier—and you'll read over and over in this book—this isn't an individual problem. Employers must step up with solutions if we are going to make real progress; Greenwood shares practical and useful strategies that leaders can apply.

You shouldn't feel alone in your attempts to avoid or recover from burnout. Some of the best approaches likely involve others. For example, you might consider forming support groups with colleagues. I've long been part of a group of women at *Harvard Business Review* that does just this. You might establish or join an employee resource group. Or you might work with HR to find ways to set realistic and healthy expectations for your role.

When my daughter was two years old, I was talking with a colleague who had older kids. I expressed a desire to land on the ideal work schedule, childcare situation, and balance of household chores with my spouse so I could get to a point where it just feels right. She smiled knowingly and told me it would probably never feel right. As devastating as that was to hear, she also gave me some great advice: Just aim for feeling OK and never, ever forget to prioritize yourself.

She was correct, of course. There is no faultless balance or magic spot on the seesaw where it all feels perfect, or even right. That's true for working moms and everyone else, too. No matter how you visualize your life—a seesaw in balance, a disorganized pile of cards, or something else entirely—you've taken the first step toward overcoming overwork by picking up this book. By better understanding where overwork comes from and how it impacts you and then putting in the time and effort to prevent (or recover from) burnout, take control of your workload, and carve out time for yourself, you can find a sense of equanimity, which is not only possible but crucial.

The Problem with Overwork

1

What's Really Holding Women Back?

by Robin J. Ely and Irene Padavic

A s scholars of gender inequality in the workplace, we are routinely asked by companies to investigate why they are having trouble retaining women and promoting them to senior ranks. It's a pervasive problem. Women made remarkable progress accessing positions of power and authority in the 1970s and 1980s, but that progress slowed considerably in the 1990s and has stalled completely in this century.

Ask people *why* women remain so dramatically underrepresented, and you will hear from the vast majority a lament—an unfortunate but inevitable "truth"—that goes something like this: High-level jobs require extremely long hours, women's devotion to family makes it impossible for them to put in those hours, and their careers suffer as a result. We call this explanation the work/family narrative. In a 2012 survey of more than 6,500 Harvard Business School alumni from many different industries, 73% of men and 85% of women invoked it to explain women's stalled advancement. Believing this explanation doesn't mean it's true, however, and our research calls it seriously into question.

We heard this explanation a few years ago from a global consulting firm that, having had no success with off-the-shelf solutions, sought our help in understanding how its culture might be hampering its women employees. The firm recruits from elite colleges and MBA programs and ranks near the top of lists of prestigious consultancies, but like most other professional services firms, it has few female partners.

We worked with the firm for 18 months, during which time we interviewed 107 consultants—women and men, partners, and associates. Virtually everybody resorted to some version of the work/family narrative to explain the paucity of female partners. But as we reported last year with our colleague Erin Reid, the more time we spent with people at the firm, the more we found that their explanations didn't correspond with the data.[1] Women weren't held back because of trouble balancing the competing demands of work and family—men, too, suffered from the balance problem and nevertheless advanced. Women were held back because, unlike men, they were encouraged to take accommodations, such as going part-time and shifting to internally facing roles, which derailed their careers. The real culprit was a general culture of overwork that hurt both men and women and locked gender inequality in place.

What People Told Us—and What the Data Showed

On several dimensions, the firm's data revealed a reality very different from the story employees told us—and were telling themselves. The disconnects we observed made us question why the story had such a powerful grip—even on the firm's data-minded analysts, who should have recognized it as a fiction.

Consider retention. Although one of the firm's motives for reaching out to us was that it wanted help addressing "women's higher turnover rate," when we took a careful look at its data for the preceding three years, we discovered virtually no difference in turnover rates for women and men.

Another area in which the firm's narrative didn't line up with the data was recognizing only women's devotion to their families: Whereas firm members attributed distress over work/family conflict primarily to women, we found that many men were suffering, too. "I was traveling three days a week and seeing my children once or twice a week for 45 minutes before they went to bed," one told us. He recalled a particularly painful Saturday when he told his son he couldn't come to his soccer game. "He burst into tears," the man said. "I wanted to quit then and there." Two-thirds of the associates we talked to who were fathers reported this kind of work/family conflict, but only one was taking accommodations to ease it.

Firm leaders had created accommodations (going part-time or shifting to internal-facing roles), which relieved some work/family balance problems, but that relief failed to translate to better outcomes for women. The problem was that employees who took advantage of them—virtually all of whom were women—were stigmatized and saw their careers derailed. The upshot for women at the individual level was sacrifices in power, status, and income; at the collective level, it meant the continuation of a pattern in which powerful positions remained the purview of men. Perversely, in its attempt to solve the problem of women's stalled advancement, the firm was perpetuating it.

We also found incongruities within the work/family rhetoric itself. Take the way this man summed up the problem: "Women are going to have kids and not want to work, or they are going to have kids and might want to work but won't want to travel every week and live the lifestyle that consulting requires, of 60- or 70-hour weeks." Resolute in his conviction that women's personal preferences were the obstacle to their success, he was unable to account for such anomalies as women with no children, whose promotion record was no better than that of mothers. In his calculation, *all* women were mothers, a conflation that was common in our interviews. Women without children figured nowhere in people's remarks, perhaps because they contradict the work/family narrative.

In a final disconnect, many of those we spoke with described experiences that called into question the work/family narrative's foundational premise: that 24/7 work schedules are unavoidable. They talked about devoting long hours to practices that were costly and unnecessary, chief among them overselling and overdelivering. We heard many stories of partners who, as one associate put it, "promise the client the moon" without thinking of how much time and energy it takes to deliver on such promises. The pitch goes like this, he explained: "We'll do X, Y, and Z, and we're going to do it all in half the time that you think it should take." Clients are wowed and can't wait to sign up, he told us.

Associates felt pressured to go along with these demands for overwork because they wanted to stand out as stars amid their highly qualified colleagues. "We do these crazy slide decks that take hours and hours of work," one said. "It's this attitude of, 'I'm going to kill the client with a 100-slide deck.' But the client can't use all that!" Another associate ruefully described all the weekends she had devoted to these sorts of tasks. "I just worked really, really hard," she told us, "and sacrificed family stuff, sacrificed my health for it, and at the end of the day, I look back on it, 'Well, did we really have to do that? Probably not.'"

We pointed out these disconnects to the firm's leaders, challenging the work/family narrative as oversimplified and offering a broader, more-nuanced, and data-driven explanation: What really held women back was the crushing culture of overwork at the firm. The unnecessarily long hours were detrimental to everyone, we explained, but they disproportionately penalized women because, unlike men, many of them take accommodations, which exact a steep career price.

All this led us to what we felt was an inescapable conclusion: For the firm to address its gender problem, it would have to address its long-hours problem. And the way to start would be to stop overselling and overdelivering.

The leaders reacted negatively to this feedback. They continued to maintain that women were failing to advance because they had difficulty balancing work and family, and they insisted that any solution had to target women specifically. Unable to convince them otherwise, we were at a loss for how to help, and the engagement effectively ended.

But we kept thinking about the situation. The firm's leaders were smart, empirically minded, and well-meaning, and yet they had dismissed the data and clung reflexively to an empirically dubious belief in the work/family narrative. As thoughtful as they were, it was a puzzle why they continued to rely on a "solution" that only perpetuated the problem.

The firm was not atypical in this regard. Research shows that a 24/7 culture creates discontent for women and men alike and that the "accommodations" solution, ironically, tends to derail the careers of highly qualified women, leaving companies' senior ranks depleted of some of their brightest female stars. Studies show an additional irony: Long hours don't raise productivity. In fact, they have been associated with decreases in performance and increases in sick-leave costs.

Considering those downsides, we asked: Why do companies continue on the same work-life balance path and disregard the possibility of instituting more-humane work hours?

We suspected that in the answer lay something profound but hidden—not just at our client firm but in corporate culture generally. Perhaps the work/family narrative is so pervasive and tenacious because it feeds into an elaborate system of social and psychological defenses that protect both women and men from the disturbing emotions that arise from the demand for long work hours. We decided to investigate.

Unconscious Psychological Defenses and Universal Beliefs

We returned to our interviews, this time paying special attention not only to *what* interviewees had said (or hadn't) but also to *how* they had said it. The exercise was illuminating. Consciously or unconsciously, virtually all the employees we had talked to revealed that they were emotionally conflicted by the firm's relentless demand for 24/7 availability and the daily choices that this demand forced them to make between family and work. The unease thus created set the stage for protective measures to kick in—measures that would keep the firm's leaders from having to face up to the devil's choice they were handing their employees, and employees from having to face up to the price of whichever choice they made.

The linchpin of those protective measures was a belief in women's natural fitness for family and in men's for work. At the employee level, they appeared as unconscious psychological defense mechanisms that reinforced the gendered work/family split. At the organizational level, they emerged as the universally held belief in the work/family narrative and in the form of policies that, as with accommodations, effectively took women off the partnership path. These employee-level and firm-level dynamics operated together to create the firm's social defense system.

All parties benefited from these measures in the short run. Firm leaders could deflect responsibility for the lack of women partners on the grounds that it was inescapable. Employees could make some semblance of peace with their decisions: Men could justify as inevitable the sacrifices they'd made in ratcheting up at work, and women could justify as natural the sacrifices they'd made in ratcheting down. And all the while, the firm's long-hours culture remained unchallenged.

But as with all defensive maneuvers, this social defense system didn't fully work. Conflict relegated to the unconscious merely hides; it isn't resolved, and anxieties continually poke through to conscious awareness, experienced differently among women than among men.

The Problem for Men

In a long-hours work culture, men have one primary identity: that of an ideal worker, fully committed and fully available. To fit this image, they must adopt the psychological stance of "my job is all-important." Nonwork identities, no matter how personally meaningful, become contingent and secondary. Naturally, this imperative to be an ideal worker generates internal conflict, especially for parents.

The men we talked to clearly felt guilty about how little time they spent with their families. They spoke poignantly about their deep emotional attachment to them, told us how much they regretted the time spent away from them, and described in heart-wrenching detail their interactions with disappointed children.

Men employed one key psychological tactic to manage these emotions: They split off their guilt and sadness, projected those feelings onto women at the firm, and identified with their feelings there, at a bit of a remove. Consider the psychological jujitsu one man performed as he drew on the work/family narrative to explain women's lack of advancement in the firm. "I believe deeply in my heart and soul that women encounter different challenges," he said. "There's the collusion of society that it's the woman who takes the extended maternity leave, and there are some biological imperatives, too. When my first child was born, I got to carry her from the delivery room to the nursery. It's almost like I could feel the chemicals releasing in my brain. I fell so chemically, deeply, in love with my daughter. I couldn't imagine a world without her. I mean, here it was in [just] the first eight minutes of her life. So I can understand, 'How can I possibly give this up and go back to work?'"

But back to work he went. And what was his takeaway from this emotionally charged experience? A sense that he better understood the difficulties *women* face in trying to balance work and family! To banish his guilt and sadness about returning to his highly demanding workweeks, he projected his intense emotional experience onto the women at the firm—a move that allowed him to let go of those feelings while still identifying with them.

Let's unpack his story. He started with a distinction between women and men, linking motherhood to biology. It is women, not men, he suggested, who have the parenting experience. He abruptly changed course to speak about his own intensely emotional and biologically determined parenting experience but then changed course again, distancing himself from that experience and projecting it onto women. In effect, he was saying, "I was having this experience, but it was transient, and now that I've sampled it, now that I've been a tourist in this emotional land, I have a way to understand what is happening to women." The emotions he had experienced, in other words, were no longer his. They now belonged to women.

At that point he shifted the conversation to the male-dominated world of work. He told us about his time in the beer industry, a domain that, as he put it, consists of "men slapping each other on the back and talking about golf and s--- like that." In his telling, there was no room in this domain for the emotional experience of parenting, which he implicitly relegated to the world of women. Men and women, he said, just have different commitments to work and family. "I can't think of a single instance," he told us, "where the fella took a six-month paternity leave to care for the baby while mom went back to work."

This man was not alone in setting up women as the organizational bearers of distress about curtailed family time. That psychological defense gave many men at the firm the illusion of a fulfilled life and enabled them to perform as the committed workers the firm valorized. But the defense was only a Band-Aid; reality—the on-the-ground, relentless demands of family—was not so easily banished.

The Problem for Women

Women experience a different psychic tension. According to the work/family narrative and broader cultural notions, their commitment to family is primary by nature, so their commitment to work *has* to be secondary. They are expected to embrace an intensive, "my family is all-important" approach to parenting, a stance encouraged by the firm's readily accessible accommodations. But a family-first stance comes at a significant cost to their careers and flies in the face of their professional ambitions.

Most of the firm's women had tasted professional success and resisted the idea that they belonged at home, which made this tension especially acute. They willingly complied with the family-devotion schema but struggled openly with the idea of splitting off the work component of their identities.

That ambivalence is clear in the account of one mother, who talked about her inability to shirk responsibilities on the home front despite having a family-oriented husband. "There's just a difference between the way a mother and a father look at their kids and the sense of responsibility that they feel," she told us. "I feel my male counterparts can more easily disconnect from what's happening at home. . . . If I did sort of disconnect, things wouldn't fall apart, but I wouldn't feel good about it, so it's just not going to happen." Yet her work commitment was also strong, leaving her at a loss for knowing whether her family responsibilities would allow her the space to develop professionally. "I know I'll fall down from time to time," she said. "I know I need to learn. . . . I don't doubt myself. . . . It's more from a place of needing to learn and needing to grow. I doubt myself generally in being able to honor that while also honoring the commitments I've made to my family. That is a constant worry." The ambivalence she felt about her career is on full display here. She embraced her family identity but was unwilling to relinquish her work identity, which is why she could say that she didn't doubt herself but then go on to say that she did.

Many other women at the firm similarly struggled with the work/family narrative's injunction to reject the role of ambitious professional. This meant that they weren't able to reap all its psychological benefits as a social defense. They willingly complied with the cultural dictate that they become the primary family caregiver, allowing men to identify vicariously with that split-off aspect of themselves—but they didn't shed their work identities. Thus the psychological resolution that men found, having made the "right" choice in fully committing themselves to a work identity, was unavailable to women, who had made the "wrong" choice in not fully committing themselves to a family identity. Working women in this situation are left with identities constructed as contradictory, forcing them to constantly assess whether they should ratchet down their career aspirations.

Adding to this tension at the firm were regular reminders that women were in the wrong place by being at work instead of at home—"push" factors that women had to withstand if they wanted to retain their work identities as ambitious professionals.

The Power of "Push" Factors

One particularly strong push factor that women encounter is work/family accommodations. Going part-time or shifting to internally facing roles provides an enticing off-ramp from the path of overwork, but those moves stigmatize women and derail their careers. Female associates at the firm who took accommodations generally fell off the track to partner; female partners who took them veered away from the route to real power.

Many women at the firm described having to resist a second push factor: the pressure to give up what they saw as their relational style in favor of the hard-charging "masculine" style the firm venerated in client interactions. One female partner told us how an early mentor warned that relying on her well-honed relationship-building skills would communicate to prospective clients that "you don't have a lot going on between your ears." In other words, her relational skill set didn't cut the mustard. Such assessments loosened women's identification with work while affirming a style more commonly associated with men, further encouraging women to step back.

A third push factor was the poor reputation of female partners with children, whose mothering was roundly condemned. These were formidable women who had held fast to their professional identities and achieved much recognition and success—achievements contradicting the idea that it is impossible to meet the demands of both work and family. One could imagine their being held up as exemplars, but we heard them routinely described as bad mothers—"horrible" women who were not "positive role models of working moms." For junior women facing decisions about being good mothers and having success-ful careers, such condemnation implies that professional commitment exacts a terrible cost.

With these push factors constantly reminding women that they don't really belong in the workplace, it's no won-der that women are often ambivalent about their career commitments. When faced with the long-hours problem, they find themselves on the horns of a dilemma: If they respond to the pull of family by taking accommodations, they undermine their status at work, but if they refuse accommodations in favor of their professional ambitions, they undermine their status as good mothers. Thus they are positioned to be seen as subpar performers or subpar mothers—or both. This dilemma leaves the culture of overwork intact, allows firms to deflect responsibility for women's stalled advancement, and locks gender inequality in place. Women are the ones who have a work/family problem to sort out, the story goes, and that's just the way it is.

. . .

Social defense systems are insidious. They divert attention from a core anxiety-provoking problem by introducing a less-anxiety-provoking one that can serve as a substitute focus. At our client firm, the core problem was the impossibly long work hours, and the substitute problem was the firm's inability to promote women. By presenting work/family accommodations as the solution to the substitute problem, the firm added to an invisible and self-reinforcing social defense system—one that cloaked inefficient work practices in the rhetoric of necessity while perpetuating gender disparities. This move gave firm leaders an unresolvable and therefore always available problem to worry about, which in turn allowed everybody to avoid confronting the core problem. As a result, two strongly held ideologies supporting the status quo remained in place: Long work hours are necessary, and women's stalled advancement is inevitable.

Our findings align with a growing consensus among gender scholars: What holds women back at work is not some unique challenge of balancing the demands of work and family but rather a general problem of overwork that prevails in contemporary corporate culture.

Women and men alike suffer as a result. But women pay higher professional costs. If we want to solve this problem, we must reconsider what we're willing to allow the workplace to demand of all employees. Such a reconsideration is possible. As individual families and employees push back against overwork, they will pave the way for others to follow. And as more research shows the business advantage of reasonable hours, some employers will come to question the wisdom of grueling schedules. If and when those forces gain traction, neither women nor men will feel the need to sacrifice the home or the work domain, demand for change will swell, and women may begin to achieve workplace equality with men.

Adapted from an article in Harvard Business Review, *March–April 2020 (product #R2002C).*

2

Five Harmful Ways Women Feel They Must Adapt at Work

by Deepa Purushothaman, Lisen Stromberg, and Lisa Kaplowitz

Women in leadership are soldiering on. While 49% of executive women considered leaving their jobs last year, only 8% actually did, according to a recent study by the nonprofit Women in Revenue.[1] This might seem like good news if you're a company leader eager to retain some of the most highly coveted talent on your payroll, but for the women themselves, there is a high cost to staying put.

In our respective (predominately U.S.-based) research, we have spoken to and surveyed thousands of high-performing professional women. On the surface, these women appear to have arrived. They're role models, company leaders, and pillars of their communities. But as we delved deeper, many of them, particularly women of color, are in crisis, struggling to live up to the demands of the ideal worker and within the constraints of a workplace not designed with them in mind. Trying to do it all and be it all leaves these women with debilitating health issues, disproportionate workloads, and pressure to perform at all costs. As one senior executive shared, "The higher I go, the more I hurt."

The women we interviewed have been taught to accept and adapt to the business cultures around them. As one Asian American woman executive shared, "Denial is the only way I can survive and do the job I was hired to do." Our research reveals five maladaptations most women have adopted to rise in corporate America. We chose to call these behaviors "maladaptations" because we see them as harmful adaptations rather than positive, helpful modifications or coping strategies. Each one on its own is detrimental to women's mental and physical well-being, but unfortunately, we found that most women adopt many of these behaviors, which further compounds their impact.

Women need to retire these maladaptations, but more importantly, company leaders need to be aware of them and redesign their cultures to enable their women leaders to thrive, not just survive. Here's what to look out for.

Maladaptation 1: I Need to Be Perfect

Study after study has revealed that women are viewed by both men *and* other women as having lower leadership potential and being less competent than men with similar skills and backgrounds.[2] Given the bias against them, the women we interviewed felt they had to be perfect to reach their seats of power. This leads to hypervigilance and extreme self-criticism. Even when things are going well, these women fear the other shoe will drop at any time: They're constantly on guard and in fight-or-flight mode at work. "I feel like people around me are just waiting for me to fail," one leader told us. "I find myself working harder to ensure nothing—absolutely nothing—goes wrong."

Our research revealed that this tendency toward perfectionism presents more severely for women of color (WOC), who have been told—and who have internalized—that they need to work at least twice as hard, if not harder, than everyone else to even get to the table. Sofia, a Latina woman and public board director (name changed to protect identity), shared:

> *Even at this level of my career, I spend hours prepping for meetings. I will write out questions and do research well beyond what the other board members are doing because I know [they] question my being here. I see it during breaks and even between*

meetings. My difference is so visible I have to be perfect and overcompensate by overpreparing.

As the "only" in the room, many women, and particularly WOC, believe their success or failure will serve as a generalization for the success or failure of their entire cohort. Ronnie, a Black woman from the Midwest, said it best when she explained:

When I joined my company, I knew I was the only Black person in my division. But after six months, I now know I am the only one in the entire company. I feel such a responsibility for making sure I represent Black people in a strong way to my white colleagues because I am the only Black person some of them have ever met in real life.

Maladaptation 2: I Need to Fit In to Rise

Many women at the top have learned that in order to rise, they must assimilate. These women feel a pressure to conform and give up parts of their core identity to advance professionally. Many women talked about sitting in seats of power but not actually feeling powerful. One woman told us, "I think so deeply about the image

I want to construct with what I share about my life. I have only recently put up pictures of my kids at work because I didn't see my peers doing it." Another senior director shared, "Our leadership is made up of white men. I feel a need to blend in, not stand out right now. I know everything I do is being watched."

WOC felt additional pressure to leave aside aspects of their ethnic and cultural identities and often went to great lengths to hide parts of their personal lives that might make them appear different from their peers. An immigrant from Latin America told us, "I didn't bring in anything that spoke to the country where I was born or the culture I was brought up in. My accent already draws attention to the fact I am different; I didn't want to add any more to that difference in case it would hurt me in getting to the next level."

Concepts like executive presence and professionalism were often full of coded messages the women internalized, causing them to edit their behaviors and how they presented themselves. As one woman described, "I struggle with the idea of 'professionalism.' It feels like a white construct used to judge if I belong. Yet, I know it is how I get evaluated, so I do it."

And yet, despite their efforts to assimilate, many women told us they had been passed over for promotion, and they learned the reason was "fit." Mattie, a CFO of a public company, shared:

I was up for a promotion and promised it was mine. And then all of a sudden, I didn't get it and found out only when the announcement was made. Even though I had the requisite experience and had stepped into the role by doing parts of the job already, the position went to one of the other men on the team. When I pushed my leaders on why this happened, they said there was some question about my long-term "fit."

Maladaptation 3: I Need to Sacrifice to Succeed

All of the women we spoke to, especially those of color, were producing and engaging beyond their formal scope of work. Whether it's through mentoring, DEI commitments, retention discussions, or recruiting other talent from diverse communities, high-achieving women take on significant extra responsibilities. Because they're often the "only," these women are asked to do more, particularly in an effort to help other women. In most cases, they struggle to say no or negotiate and end up taking on the extra tasks without any clear incentive or additional compensation, and often at the expense of doing work that would more directly lead to career advancement.

Not surprisingly, the women we met were exhausted—and we can relate. They're sacrificing their well-being and physically feeling the stress from work. They're ignoring the signs their bodies are giving them in order to perform and achieve: signs like headaches, adrenal fatigue, skin rashes, heart palpitations, stomach pain, and fertility challenges. For most senior women, it's their health that finally draws attention to the need for change.

While all of the high-achieving women we interviewed are burned out, our research revealed that the women of color are also traumatized. In addition to the exhaustion from trying to be perfect, assimilating into a work structure that doesn't truly value what they bring, and taking on the additional work of being the "only," WOC are dealing with trauma related to racism and suffer deeply from microaggressions in the workplace. Many of the women we met believed they must tolerate this behavior to be in corporate spaces. Shilpa illustrated this so clearly when she said:

> *I have spent the last few years wondering why I was so exhausted and my body was failing me. I have been to the doctor many times. I'm the only WOC at the VP level, and I was convinced I needed to grow thicker skin. When I finally decided to leave my job, so many women from the company reached out to me. They were fed up with the culture, too. It never occurred to me how many of the other women I know are suffering.*

Maladaptation 4: I Need to Do It Alone

With the myth of meritocracy still infused across corporate America, most of the women told us they've felt forced to go it alone in their rise to the top. One woman, Mia, shared, "I think I was taught I had to go at it alone, but I am not sure where I picked that up, or why I am proud of the fact I have done it alone." These women have climbed the ladder with determination and find themselves sitting in coveted seats. They're finally at the table, but they have few trusted advisers or truly safe spaces where they feel seen and accepted. Their professional male mentors don't understand their full experience, and many of the women haven't had time or space to build outside relationships because of the demands of their career and family life.

This pattern becomes most apparent when things go wrong. Additionally, many women find themselves promoted to their first leadership positions during times of crisis, which is likely to set them up for failure (this is known as the "glass cliff" phenomenon). In times of strife—either personal or professional—these women feel how alone they are. When Mia was passed over for a transfer to a new department with a bigger role, she was told she needed more time to grow her confidence. She shared:

> *No one ever said that to me until I pushed for an explanation. I didn't realize until I was part of your*

group discussion how prevalent this type of feedback was for women at my level. I spent months wondering if I had misread the cues or if something in how I presented myself had changed.

This issue presents as more acute with the WOC we work with—because there are fewer WOC in senior positions, there's more "aloneness." Sonia faced an incident of racism at work, and after six weeks of agonizing over whether to take formal action, she finally filed a complaint. The mostly male, white team members around her were unsupportive and conveyed both directly and indirectly that she wasn't being a team player. Sonia struggled as the issue was investigated, and she realized how few advocates she had to support her in the process. Her friends and family tried to listen, but it became glaringly clear how few professional WOC she could call for support and advice.

Our research told us that many high-achieving women spent their time focused on "arriving." In the process, they haven't had time to build full, robust relationships or support mechanisms either in or outside of work.

Maladaptation 5: Success Means Having It All

When the concept of having it all came into vogue in the 1980s, it was not intended to mean that women work outside the home *and* do all the laundry and cooking and diaper changing. Yet the underlying social norms have resulted in women doing more of the housework and childcare than men, regardless of who has a higher-paying job. On top of that, 70% of high-earning men have stay-at-home spouses, while only 22% of high-earning women do.[3]

Combine this with the conflicting struggle of trying to embody both the ideal worker, ideal partner, and ideal mother. Many of the women we interviewed struggle with feeling that they're "enough." In their rise to the top, high-achieving women told us in story after story that they spent so much time proving themselves at work, their personal lives suffered. Married women told us they didn't have that same level of energy for their households or their marriages. Susan, a senior woman in banking, told us, "I have spent 20 years climbing the ranks to SVP. I make more than my husband, and I know that is a growing issue for him; I just avoid it." Single women explained that it was hard to find significant others because so much of their time was spent at work or thinking about work.

This loss of balance makes their success, no matter how impressive on paper, feel hollow and stifling, as though it were something to endure and prop up, rather than celebrate and embody. One woman described:

> *I know I am a success on paper, but my life feels like a failure when I look at my marriage and how much*

energy I have available for my kids. I am running on empty, and I feel like I am just trying to keep everything afloat. I run from one problem to the next without enough time for anything. I'm finally asking myself, is it worth it?

. . .

The toxic behaviors these maladaptations give rise to rarely work for any of us. And maladaptations don't just impact women; men have been forced to create their own set of coping mechanisms in their rise to the top.

For women, it's time we evolve beyond these maladaptations and (re)claim our agency. Rather than maintain the status quo, company leaders need to collectively change their acceptance and tolerance of maladaptations and reject the binary of "leaning in" or "leaning out" as the makers or breakers of success. Instead, they need to recognize that women need to lean within and listen to their own wisdom about what it means to be healthy, whole, and successful. Women can't just stop these maladaptations and survive on their current tracks; companies need to evolve, too.

Adapted from "5 Harmful Ways Women Feel They Must Adapt in Corporate America," on hbr.org, October 31, 2022 (product #H07B5E).

3

When Your Career Becomes Your Whole Identity

by Janna Koretz

D
anielle (name changed to protect identity), a partner at a major Boston law firm, was due at the office, but instead, she was curled on her bathroom floor, in her pajamas, crying into a towel.

It began slowly, in a meeting with a particularly pushy client, when a thought bubbled up in her mind: "Why the hell am I even here?" From that moment, she noticed that her impatience, unhappiness, and frustration with her job grew deeper, until all at once, she realized: She didn't find happiness or fulfillment in her work—and maybe she never had.

For someone who had built her entire idea of herself around her career, this thought sent Danielle into an existential crisis. Who was she, if not a high-powered lawyer? Had she wasted so many years working for nothing? Would she have had more friends and a happier family if she hadn't spent all those nights at the office?

Danielle's story is not uncommon. Many people with high-pressure jobs find themselves unhappy with their careers, despite working hard their whole lives to get to their current position. Hating your job is one thing—but what happens if you identify so closely with your work that hating your job means hating yourself?

Psychologists use the term "enmeshment" to describe a situation where the boundaries between people become blurred, and individual identities lose importance. Enmeshment prevents the development of a stable, independent sense of self. Danielle—like many in high-pressure jobs—had become enmeshed not with another person, but with her career.

As a psychologist, I specialize in mental health challenges associated with high-pressure careers. People like Danielle show up in my office every day—so often, in fact, I had to build a company, Azimuth Psychological, to focus on serving their needs. A particular confluence of high achievement, intense competitiveness, and a culture of overwork has caught many in a perfect storm of career enmeshment and burnout. Over the years, we've found that these issues interact in such complex ways with people's identity, personality, and emotions that it often requires full-on psychological therapy to address them successfully.

So, what is it about high-pressure careers that too often lead to mental health issues like those Danielle faced?

The work culture in many high-pressure fields often rewards working longer hours with raises, prestige, and promotions. Danielle found that spending more and more time in the office (or tethered to her corporate iPhone) was the price she had to pay for her rapid rise through the firm. However, when you engage in any intense activity for the great majority of your waking hours, that activity will tend to become more and more central to your identity—if only because it has displaced other activities and relationships with which you might identify.

Certain careers or career achievements are often highly valued in an individual's family or community. Danielle's parents had both been lawyers, and while they never explicitly pushed Danielle into a legal career, they had high expectations for her professional and financial achievements. When career success is seen as the ultimate life goal, individuals can feel disconnected from their family and peers if they fail to (or simply choose not to) achieve a certain level of professional success. This fear of failure and isolation drives people to center their lives on achieving what is expected of them. This intense focus and drive, however, forces their identities to ultimately become synonymous with their work.

When high-pressure jobs are paired with a big paycheck, individuals can find themselves launched into a new socioeconomic class. It wasn't just the homes, cars, vacations, and gadgets that Danielle suddenly couldn't live without—it was the friends, the dinner parties, the charity galas. Our identities are highly influenced by how we present ourselves to others. When someone forms an identity focused on wealth, achievement, and influence, they tie themselves to that high-paying career that got them there.

Even for those who don't burn out, constructing one's identity closely around a career is a risky move. Companies and entire industries struggle and go under. Age discrimination can make it especially difficult for those in the mid to late stages of their career to find a suitable role in their field after a layoff. No matter how it happens, becoming disconnected from a career that forms the foundation of your identity can lead to bigger issues, such as depression, anxiety, substance use, and loneliness.

So how do you know if your identity has become enmeshed with your career? Consider the following questions:

- How much do you think about your job outside the office? Is your mind frequently consumed with work-related thoughts? Is it difficult to participate in conversations that are not about your work?

- How do you describe yourself? How much of this description is tied up in your job, title, or company? Are there any other ways you would describe yourself? How quickly do you tell people you've just met about your job?

- Where do you spend most of your time? Has anyone ever complained to you that you are in the office too much?

- Do you have hobbies outside work that do not directly involve your work-related skills and abilities? Are you able to consistently spend your time exercising other parts of your brain?

- How would you feel if you could no longer continue in your profession? How distressing would this be to you?

If these questions cause you to worry about the degree to which your job has influenced your identity, there are things you can do to initiate change. You can accomplish these on your own, or with the help of a therapist who understands the challenges faced by individuals in high-pressure careers.

Free up time. Delegate tasks at work to free up time, and (crucially) fill that time with nonwork-related activities. This could mean relying more heavily on your coworkers, hiring a virtual assistant, or advocating for an intern or additional colleague to help with tasks. Effective delegation requires giving up some control of exactly how the work is executed, which in itself is a healthy exercise in communication and acceptance.

Start small. For your new activities outside work, start small and try out some hobbies you've had your eye on. You don't have to commit to anything long term; the idea is to start exploring new things you might want to integrate into your life and your identity. For example, if you want to exercise more, don't sign up for a marathon— just start walking to work or taking a gym break during lunch once or twice a week. Small changes like this are easier to stick with and over time can result in a virtuous cycle of improvement and commitment.

Rebuild your network. Reach out to friends and family to revitalize your social circles. You'll end up having fun while also establishing a support network for yourself. Even just reaching out by text, email, or phone to catch up with people you haven't spoken to in a while can help strengthen relationships. It doesn't take much; recent research on adult friendships has shown that having just three to five close friends is associated with the highest levels of life satisfaction.[1]

Decide what's important to you. Establish and review your principles and values. What is most important to you? Think about what you care about in life, and let those priorities guide you toward what's next. Therapists often use a process called "values clarification" to help their clients think through what matters most to them. This process involves reflecting on your desired direction in areas like relationships, community, careers, and parenting, then ranking them in terms of importance to you. While formal worksheets can be helpful, you can start by creating and updating a running list on your phone as you think about what is most important to you.

Look beyond your job title. Consider reframing your relationship to your career not simply in terms of your company or title, but in terms of your skills that could be used across different contexts. For example, many psychotherapists who burn out on seeing clients find that their skills translate well to human resources management or guidance counseling.

While identifying closely with your career isn't necessarily bad, it makes you vulnerable to a painful identity crisis if you burn out, get laid off, or retire. Individuals in these situations frequently suffer anxiety, depression, and despair. By reclaiming some time for yourself and diversifying your activities and relationships, you can build a more balanced and robust identity in line with your values.

Adapted from "What Happens When Your Career Becomes Your Whole Identity," on hbr.org, December 26, 2019 (product #H05C4S).

4

Resisting the Pressure to Overwork

by Alice Boyes

Few of us want to overwork. Even when our jobs feel meaningful, we'd prefer to work to live, not live to work. We benefit from also devoting time to other interests and hobbies, family and friends, leisure, and learning not related to our professions. Those are meaningful to us too.

Still, it's easy to get sucked (or suckered) into working too hard. To avoid this, you'll need well-articulated strategies. Try these.

Understand That Overwork Is Not Necessary for Success

If you buy into that thinking, even just a tiny bit, you won't be able to resist triggers, like others telling you about their overworking. This social pressure will activate your anxiety, with all the attendant emotional and physical reactions.

Here's an example. Another author recently told me how many podcast interviews they'd done to support their book launch. It was far more than I had done, and this sent me into a spiral of worry. Even hours later, my heart rate remained elevated and my mind kept drifting back to it.

To avoid the temptation to keep up with vocal overworkers like that author, you need to radically reject the idea that such behavior is required or even beneficial. In my case, I literally had to say to myself, "That person believes overworking is necessary for success. I don't believe that."

If a situation continues to trigger you, consider using even more compassionate self-talk. For example, "I feel anxious that if I don't buy into their assumptions, I'm going to fail. My success is important to me, so that's scary. But I'm going to remind myself about how I can do my best work through methods that don't involve overworking."

Be Clear on Your Values

As that author talked about their many podcast appearances, the tone wasn't "I've connected with so many amazing interviewers, and it's been so interesting and enriching." It was more like "I'm grinding it out. Isn't it a pain to have to do that?"

I never want to feel that way going into interviews. I want to approach with curiosity, learn something from the interviewers, and be prompted to think about ideas differently or express my own thoughts in ways I haven't before.

Beyond that, I also value efficiency. Yes, I could try to be a guest on 100 podcasts. But it seems far smarter to identify the 20 most likely to drive book sales and then another five to 10 that seem interesting, to introduce some randomness and serendipity into the process.

It's important to specifically identify your values. Sure, most of us can agree that things like equality, justice, efficiency, generosity, bravery, autonomy, challenge, cooperation, and adventure are good. However, we differ in our priorities—our most important values—and what makes us feel most like our lives and careers are meaningful and on track. For instance, if you highly value bravery, consider how you can approach your core tasks with more of it. Think not just about what you'd rather be doing than working but also your attitude and approach to finding fulfillment *in* work.

Also trust that this values-driven approach will lead to some of the outcomes that are important to you. With experience and experimentation, you'll learn to do enough in your work or career, instead of measuring achievement by the hours you're putting in.

Reject Hustle Culture. Instead Focus on Deeper Goals and Your Craft

Einstein wasn't trying to "crush it" or "kill it" at work. In fact, the behaviors and language associated with hustle culture don't typically lead to great accomplishments. What does is the pursuit of deeper, more personal goals like knowing and understanding important phenomena, solving complex problems, or making a positive impact in society. You might think about goals in more concrete terms, of course (for example, sales targets), but also consider the greater ambition that matters most to you and try to focus on the tasks and assignments that help you achieve it, jettisoning much of the rest.

Another way to step away from hustle culture—whether you're a teacher, accountant, or manager—is to reframe your job as a craft that you're trying to hone. This should make you more interested in facets of work like acquiring skills, getting feedback, and interacting with a wide range of people who can help you improve. All of these will propel you to do not more but more important work that allows you to make good on your big goals.

Learn from Role Models

Consider the people who have achieved the kind of success you want without overworking or constantly noting how swamped and exhausted they are like it's a badge of honor. (Note: this type of complaining has become normalized, but it is *not* normal. If someone is truly exhausted by their work, that's a problem that needs to be addressed.)

To be clear, I'm not talking about identifying role models who are celebrities or CEOs you admire but don't know. A more effective strategy when trying to find role models is to simply look inside and outside your professional niche. Who inspires you by doing well without overwork, hustle, or burning themselves out? What are their approaches? Can you adapt any of them to fit your values, goals, personality, and circumstances?

Ignore Requests to Overwork

Here's a very basic law of psychology: When behaviors are reinforced, they increase. When you ignore them, you might see an "extinction burst"—a short-term rise in the problematic behaviors—but then they will stop.

For example, if a colleague emails you after hours and you reply, you're encouraging more work at night. The sender will ask for more—from you and everyone else. If you instead ignore inappropriate attempts to push you to overwork, the person may for a short period of time try frenetically and in more manipulative ways to get you to comply—the extinction burst—but then they'll adapt. People are wired to learn.

If your boss is the one pressing you to overwork, that's one of the most basic signs of an abusive work culture. Make your boundaries clear, and if the behaviors don't stop, consider roles on different teams or in different organizations with managers who have more realistic expectations. As organizational psychologist Adam Grant says, "It's not your job to fix a toxic workplace from the bottom."

We all face internal and external pressure to do more. But in the pursuit of career success and fulfillment, overwork is your enemy, not your friend. These strategies can help you push back against it.

Adapted from content posted on hbr.org, May 26, 2022 (product #H0721Q).

Prevent Burnout by Working Smarter

5

Manage Your Burnout

A conversation with Mandy O'Neill

Working long hours won't necessarily burn us out, but getting too little sleep or feeling unappreciated might. Women commonly face extra stressors, like office chores or doing a "second shift" at home, that can leave us exhausted. And once we're burned out, it usually takes more than a few coffee breaks or going on vacation to feel like ourselves again.

Amy Bernstein, Nicole Torres, and Amy Gallo talked to Mandy O'Neill, an expert on workplace well-being, who explained the causes, symptoms, and repercussions of burnout. She suggested several ways to protect ourselves from experiencing it in the first place and antidotes (including laughing with your colleagues).

AMY BERNSTEIN: Mandy, let's start by defining our terms. What do we mean when we talk about burnout?

MANDY O'NEILL: Like most things, there are as many definitions as people who are interested in burnout. A lot of academics look to Christina Maslach's 30 years of research when we think about what burnout means: emotional exhaustion, depersonalization, and a declining sense of personal accomplishment.

AMY B: What are the particular workplace stressors that lead most to burnout?

MANDY: Just as beauty is in the eye of the beholder, so too is stress. Perceptions matter. Something that's stressful to one person might be just fine to somebody else. If we look at the stressors that crop up again and again, a few things come up. One is resources, which include money, promotions, and benefits. But they also include psychological elements. I've studied hospitals and health-care systems that are resource-rich and, unsurprisingly, are also places where I see the least amount of burnout. There could be a visionary CEO or a wonderful client population. There could be a great financial bottom line. But these are organizations that have the resources to support the staff. This includes not only pay, but the ability to do things in your free time that matter to you, for example, taking time out of your workday to participate in a project involving pet therapy or whatever your interests are. It doesn't necessarily include money; it includes time and autonomy. In contrast, organizations that are resource-poor have some of the worst levels of burnout. The two are strongly related. This might entail terrible physical working conditions, not enough staff, or not enough resources to do the work and do it well. It could also include a cutthroat, bottom-line, results-oriented culture, where the funding's not coming through, the innovations aren't there, and the CEO is cutting everything possible to make the numbers with the bare minimum resources.

AMY GALLO: Can you talk about focus problems and how that might lead to burnout?

MANDY: Women have always had a second shift. They've gone home to more work. They're often the people who are responsible for the household finances and the childcare. This creates well-known problems with distraction. In the literature, we sometimes call it "cognitive load." It's knowing you must do something, but you're asked to memorize five numbers while doing it. Necessarily, that's going to cause a focus problem. Being aware of the second shift that happens outside of work and the extent to which women are taking it on might explain why you sometimes see focus problems.

NICOLE TORRES: What about the thing that everyone links to burnout—long hours.

MANDY: Long hours are definitely not all created equal, because you can have long hours filled with work that you love and long hours that make you feel like you have nothing in life besides work and it's draining to the bone. It depends on whether you're into it. Long hours per se are not the problem. It's a contributor, particularly if what you're doing in those long hours is taking you away from other things that are important to you—friends, family, relationships, health, working out—or it's work that you just don't enjoy and that you can't finish during work hours.

NICOLE: Have you felt burned out? Can you give us a sense of what it looks like?

MANDY: I have. It's one of the reasons I took my entire family and I from our home on the East Coast to the University of California, Berkeley, on sabbatical. I recognized the symptoms in myself. They grew over time, and like any good researcher, I tried to apply what we call "me-search," to myself and said, I'm feeling burnout. I probably need to do something about it.

NICOLE: What were some of your symptoms?

MANDY: In some ways, they're very close to what the literature says. I've taught so many students and had so many wonderful experiences, stories, and personal situations. (This upcoming year will be my 13th as a professor.) But I had gotten to a point where I just couldn't feel anything anymore. I looked at my students and the personal circumstances and complicating factors as just one big blur. My compassion valve had shut down. I'm a naturally warm, compassionate person, and something was wrong when I couldn't feel their pain anymore. I looked at what was going on in their lives and their complications, and it just blended together. Depersonalization was the biggest symptom for me.

AMY G: Two things seem noteworthy about your experience. One, a lack of compassion. But also, that you weren't feeling like yourself. How much is that feeling as if you don't even recognize yourself part of burnout?

MANDY: It's an interesting insight that hasn't been explored deeply. But, a big part is knowing yourself and what your own triggers are. For someone who's just not naturally compassionate, this could be their status quo. They don't have very strong emotional reactions to their work or to people. Burnout might look a little different for them. But for someone like me, who's normally emotional, effusive, and deeply compassionate, something was wrong when I couldn't feel that anymore.

AMY B: Do you think women experience burnout differently from men?

MANDY: Like most things, the internal, psychological, and emotional experience of burnout is probably pretty similar between men and women. What differs, though, is how people deal with it. We know that men and women mostly feel the same emotions and, for the most part, to the same extent. But they express them differently, and there are some emotions that are not as appropriate, let's say, for men and women to express. This is one aspect in which women actually have an advantage in that, historically speaking, it's been more acceptable for them to express a wider range of emotions in general than men. When burnout happens, women are more likely to be able to express it than men. There's another question about what happens in the workplace when they do express emotions. That's where we see a much narrower band of acceptable behaviors. But, what do you do with those emotions when you start feeling them? Men tend to suppress emotions more than women do, which is one of the worst things to do, particularly for negative emotions, because not only do they not go away, but they also crop up in other ways—in memory, interpersonal relationships, health, well-being.

NICOLE: If women can express a wider range of emotions, then what leads to women experiencing burnout differently?

MANDY: It has something to do with the burnout itself and with what they do with the burnout. We know, for example, that women are asked to do office chores like cleaning the coffee pot or being the emotional support for the colleague who's going through a rough time. There are invisible tasks that women take on because of expectations about who should be dealing with them but also, in some cases, their natural proclivities. They're taking on more at work, which probably contributes to burnout in a more comprehensive way than it does for men. At the same time, women have different opportunities for dealing with burnout because it's more acceptable for them to express vulnerability, sadness, and depression than it is for men. And interestingly, in terms of opting out, historically women have had opportunities outside of getting to the C-suite that are much more acceptable for them than for men.

AMY B: How does chronic stress fit into all this? Is it the same as burnout? Does it lead to burnout?

MANDY: Stress has a physiological profile that differs from burnout and is actually quite functional. When you have a lot of stress, your body usually starts shutting down or reminding you or giving you clues that you need to step back. You'll often get sick or tired, and your body tells you that you need to get some sleep. This is actually a very helpful thing because it's your body's way of say-ing that you need to change something, and if you're not going to change it, the body's not going to be able to perform optimally. Burnout is a little trickier because, unlike stress, people keep going, which is partly how it gets to be chronic.

AMY B: How can you head off burnout? In my own experience, I don't realize I am burned out until it's severe. How can I just avoid it altogether?

MANDY: Getting a good night's sleep before coming into the workplace is important, and being your best self (having good interpersonal relations, doing your work, performing well). There's a metaphor called the "fish in water" effect. When you're swimming, and you don't know you're in the water, it takes someone outside the fishbowl to look in and say, "Hey, that water's really dirty." That's where it's helpful to have a personal board of advisers. They could be colleagues at work, friends in your personal life, partners, or family, who can say, "You know, I've seen you go down this road," when you can't see it, because you're that fish in water.

Adapted from "Managing Burnout," Women at Work *podcast, season 3, episode 1, April 15, 2019.*

6

Burning Out? Give Yourself Permission to Dial It Back

by Kate Northrup

You've heard the stats on overwork and how huge of a health risk it is. You've read the productivity articles and books indicating that loading up your week with more work hours doesn't actually improve your results. And while the *idea* of dialing it back not only sounds appealing and is backed by significant data, giving yourself permission to do that is something else entirely.

There are many reasons why we put in more and more hours despite increasing evidence that it's not only not effective, but also shortening our lives. There's the pressure to look like a hard worker who's available at all times, especially in industries where responding to a client or your boss's needs at any time is the norm. There's the desire to get ahead and be selected for promotions, raises, and leadership opportunities. There's the cultural messaging we've received our whole lives that putting in more hours and more effort ensures our success, even though discerning what to put your effort into is far more important than blanketing your life in hard work. And it's hard to change a belief. Study after study shows us that we don't change our minds even when given new, factual information that proves our previous beliefs wrong.[1]

It's no wonder, then, that despite plenty of evidence that dialing it back is smart for both our productivity and our health, we have trouble giving ourselves permission to do it. But just because it's unusual or uncomfortable to change your work habits, it's by no means impossible.

Here are a few things that have worked for my clients and in my own personal experience to give yourself permission to dial it back.

Notice the story you're telling yourself about work

It's 6 p.m. You promised you'd be home for dinner and bedtime, but you've got a few last emails you want to get out. In these moments where you have a choice to continue your old behavior of blowing past your boundaries or commitments to parts of your life outside work, notice what story you're telling yourself about why work is more important.

Take five minutes or so to write out the story you're telling yourself and then dig deeper. If the story is that if you don't send out those last few emails, you'll be behind tomorrow, ask yourself: *Then what?* Perhaps the answer is that then you'll feel rushed to get your proposal in by the end of the week. Ask yourself again: *Then what?* Keep digging until you get to the core story. It will often be something like, "I'll lose my job and then lose everything."

Once you've reached this point, ask yourself: *Is it true?* Is it true that if you leave work at the time you said you would, you will lose your job and then lose everything else? In most situations, probably not. Our thoughts and feelings trigger our behavior, and our inner stories are interwoven with these thoughts and feelings. By taking a few minutes to interrupt your automatic thoughts, feelings, and behavior, you make it more likely that you can make a change.

Share your goal to dial it back with someone you respect

According to research from the American Psychological Association, when you share your goal with someone you perceive as having higher status or you respect, it holds you accountable for doing it because you care about their opinion of you.[2] Plus, when it comes to allowing yourself to take your foot off the brake a little, chances are one of the reasons it's hard is because you want higher-ups to see you as a dedicated, hard worker.

The person you share your goal with doesn't have to be within your company. They could be a mentor, friend, or family member who you admire for their ability to do great work while also giving themselves permission to live their life to the fullest. Beyond simply holding you accountable, they might also offer helpful guidance about how they gave themselves permission to dial it back that you can then follow.

Go all in on what matters

We tend to be very one and 10 in our thinking, telling ourselves the erroneous story that doing less in one area means doing less (or nothing) everywhere else. That's how we convince ourselves that it's not OK. That math simply does not add up.

Instead, do an 80/20 analysis and determine what 20% of tasks or projects give you 80% of the results at work. List your biggest wins at work (the results you're after, your biggest priorities, or your top goals) on one side of a piece of paper and the tasks you do on a daily basis on the left. Draw a line from each of the big wins to the tasks that were most directly responsible for that outcome. Circle the tasks that have lines drawn from them. That's your 20%.

Once you know this, you can give the most time and energy to the things that matter, and you can see the other areas where you can dial it back, delegate, or eliminate things altogether. Plus, if you know you're devoting the best of you to the things that matter at work, you'll also have an easier time shutting it down when it's time.

Fast-forward

Bronnie Ware's beautiful book, *The Top Five Regrets of the Dying*, reminds us that it's incredibly common for people, when they're on their deathbed, to wish they hadn't worked so much. When we're caught up in the daily grind, it's easy to get stuck thinking that reworking that report for the 100th time or putting in an extra two hours a day at our computer is crucial to our lives.

Instead, consider this exercise: When I feel stuck in an old pattern and have difficulty changing my behavior, I like to fast-forward and ask my 85-year-old self what she would wish I would have done at my current stage of life. Doing so allows me to see the bigger picture, rather than the deadlines or stressors that are my immediate focus at that time. You can do the same. When you zoom out and pretend you're looking back at your life, it's easier to see what's essential and what isn't.

Your ability to give yourself permission to dial it back (even just a little) has the potential to drastically improve your results and protect your health. You work hard, and you do work that matters. You deserve to achieve your goals while giving your body and mind the space they need to perform optimally as well.

Adapted from content posted on hbr.org, October 6, 2021 (product #H06M0Q).

7

Five Steps for Women to Combat Burnout

by Ellen Keithline Byrne

A s an executive coach who works with women leaders, it's not unusual for me to see the sad, worried eyes of my coaching clients as the aha moment hits, and they realize: "I have burnout."

This realization often comes as a shock. Once it's teased out and women further share their feelings of exhaustion and lack of energy for work they once loved, it becomes glaringly obvious to them. But until that point, they typically beat themselves up, their inner voice saying, "I just need to work harder! What's wrong with me?"

My business partners and I estimate that almost 20% of the women in our six-month leadership intensives are expressing some symptoms of burnout. What we know is that it's insidious and can slowly creep up on you. These clients have moved past periodic times of being stressed out into chronic stress. This occupational phenomenon clouds the mind, where a person struggles to assess their situation clearly, and they often end up berating themselves for not being good enough.

One client, a CEO in a midsize insurance company, who had been truly passionate about her work, realized she was burned out. After years of tirelessly committing her time to the business, one day, she struggled to listen to the chairman of the board when he walked into her office, whereas in the past she looked forward to their conversations. She described it as the Charlie Brown adult voice that's just "*wah, wah, wah.*" She felt exhausted when she woke up each morning and just wanted to stay home, make soup, and watch *I Love Lucy* reruns.

This description is unfortunately not unusual. Our clients often have the reputation of being driven and passionate. Yet, over time, they feel overwhelmed and struggle to identify what's wrong. Sometimes I hear them contemplate leaving their company just to find some sense of inner peace. And sometimes they don't make changes until they end up in emergency rooms or with a serious health diagnosis. This can often lead to a leave of absence or termination. Successful leaders need to know what burnout looks like and get help early.

Here is what we know:

Burnout is now considered a serious work issue, as the pace and complexity of our work environments have rapidly changed. In May 2019, the World Health Organization updated the definition of burnout as: "resulting from chronic workplace stress that has not been successfully managed."[1] This new definition is raising the awareness of burnout and strengthening its link to work. It legitimizes the need to pay attention to these occupational symptoms and find solutions that alleviate toxic work environments. The expert on burnout, Dr. Christina Maslach of the University of California, Berkeley, describes it as "a prolonged response to chronic interpersonal stressors on the job."[2]

It's no surprise that women report higher levels of burnout. One study identified gender inequalities in the workplace as a key element that's impacting occupational mental health.[3] Women were found to have lower levels of decision-making authority and were often overqualified for their roles, which ultimately leads to less satisfaction at work and a sense that they have fewer career alternatives. We see this frustration all the time, and it often manifests in beating oneself up. Women often think it's their own fault that they're not thriving.

Our concern after decades of working with women leaders is that it's getting worse. Here is what we recommend:

Determine Right Away Whether You Have Burnout, and If So, How Bad It Is

Burnout is progressive. People typically start with one or two of the following identifiers, and it usually builds from there. Maslach's research highlights three main questions to ask yourself:[4]

1. **Are you regularly physically and emotionally exhausted?** Do you feel a lack of energy and/or have trouble sleeping? Do you worry excessively? Feel more edgy? Feel sad or hopeless?

2. **Are you more cynical and detached than usual?** Do you no longer feel joy from things that used to bring you joy? Are you less interested in socializing and are you feeling less connected to people than you once did? Are you more negative than usual? Do you see the glass as half empty?

3. **Are you feeling like you're not contributing anything meaningful where you once did?** Do you feel a sense of ineffectiveness, that all of your hard work isn't actually accomplishing anything?

If you respond yes to all or several of these questions, the alarm bells should be going off. It's time to schedule an appointment with your internist, mental health professional, or a coach. These questions—especially the last two—take the concept of normal stress to the next level, in terms of how it has impacted your overall mindset.

Catch It Early. Awareness Is the First Step

This is sometimes the hardest part. We can be tough on ourselves and are often not willing to reflect on our own behavior.

Clients will often share that colleagues and friends have expressed concern that they are not themselves or that they are doing too much. But they brush it off as just needing to work harder and smarter. If you're hearing similar comments from colleagues or friends, take heed. Coming to terms with the idea that you are either in crisis or heading there soon is not easy. Examine the previous questions and be honest with yourself.

Get Support

Whether it's a good friend, family member, therapist, or coach, have someone who can challenge your thinking and give you another perspective. Once burnout has its hold on your mindset, decision-making can get fuzzy. By identifying patterns and regaining clarity on priorities, you can establish better boundaries, for instance, by delegating where necessary, by saying no to projects that do not serve you long term, and by taking better care of yourself. These steps can help you feel a sense of progress toward relieving your symptoms.

Make Your Emotional and Physical Well-Being a Priority

Put healthy eating, exercise, and a good sleep routine at the top of the list. Schedule lunch breaks and stop working at a reasonable time. Take all of your vacation days. Too many companies report that employees forgo vacation time; 27.2% of paid time off went unused in 2018.[5] And too many women tell us that they're the first ones in the office in the morning, and the last ones out at night. Reframe that "work harder" message to work smarter, which includes breaks from work to stimulate the relaxation response and dissipate the stress response. Give yourself permission to shift your mindset around what's a priority and a commitment to establishing healthy coping mechanisms to combat stress.

Examine Your Work Environment

Burnout is a result of a mismatch between the demands of the job and the available resources. In chapter 1, Robin Ely and Irene Padavic identified that "what holds women back at work is not some unique challenge of balancing the demands of work and family but rather a general problem of overwork that prevails in contemporary corporate culture."[6] The current workplace mantra of "we have to do more with less" is unsustainable. With your manager or other senior leaders, review the structure of your role, the culture of the firm, and how to support an environment where everyone thrives.

For women leaders to better respond to and adapt to our changing workplaces, it's critical that a clearer understanding of what burnout is and how it manifests is necessary. As a coach, I hope that through education, my clients will be able to catch it early, apply the coping mechanisms they've learned, and not end up with serious health issues. We should all be striving for workplaces where everyone thrives.

Adapted from "5 Steps for Women to Combat Burnout," on hbr.org, May 13, 2020 (product #H05JME).

8

Women Do More to Fight Burnout—and It's Burning Them Out

by Tiffany Burns, Jess Huang, Alexis Krivkovich, Ishanaa Rambachan, Tijana Trkulja, and Lareina Yee

Burnout is real and getting worse. The numbers are discouraging, for both men and women: 42% of women and 35% of men in corporate America felt burned out in 2021 (up from 32% and 28%, respectively, in 2020). One of three women surveyed say they have considered downshifting or leaving the workforce altogether. (In 2020, it was one in four.) These figures come from McKinsey and LeanIn.org's 2021 Women in the Workplace report, which surveyed 65,000 people in the United States.[1]

Despite their own increasing levels of burnout, our research also indicates that women are much more likely than men to take action to fight it, for example, by managing workloads of their teams; supporting diversity, equity, and inclusion efforts; and simply checking in on how employees are doing. This makes a difference: We found, for example, that when managers actively managed the workload of their team, their staff were 32% less likely to be burned out and 33% less likely to leave.

On the whole, however, companies are not recognizing or incentivizing this work—meaning they risk losing the very leaders they need right now. While 87% of companies surveyed agreed that it was "very or extremely" critical that managers support employee well-being, only a quarter do much about it.

To do better, companies must fully invest in and equip day-to-day line managers—those in the closest supervisory position to staff—for this work. In fact, people managers, especially women, are more likely to be burned out than those who do not manage people, so companies must do more to alleviate pressure and retain these employees who have stepped up to lead at a critical time.

Here are three actions companies can take to support managers' efforts in addressing burnout.

Set Companywide Norms

While many employees value the greater flexibility of remote work, a major downside is the idea that they are "always on," or available to work 24/7. This cohort, which accounts for more than a third of those in our survey, are much more likely to report being burned out.

To take pressure off managers, companies should establish basic working norms, such as putting guardrails around off-hours communications and clearly setting expectations on response time. This is not currently happening: Only one in five employees told us their company has said they don't need to respond to nonurgent requests outside traditional work hours.

Companies should also make it clear that they base evaluations on performance, not promptness in answering a late-night email. And most importantly, managers should model these behaviors: Show that it is OK to not always be on by unplugging and setting healthy boundaries.

Equip Managers with the Training and Resources to Lead

When managers support employee well-being, employees are 25% more likely to be happy at work. But companies must equip managers to be part of the solution by first raising awareness of the challenges employees face within the workplace. This can be done, for example, by providing managers with tools, such as a survey, to easily pulse-check their teams.

Companies then need to move this awareness to action, by regularly offering and promoting training and resources for managers on topics such as how to spot burnout or be an ally or an inclusive leader. Our research shows that employees who have strong allies are happier and less burned out, yet in 2021 just 14% of employees received allyship training. Managers need to be at the forefront supporting employees and modeling these positive behaviors, but there has to be clear investment from companies to indicate the strong intent to create a better workplace.

Formally Recognize the Work Managers Do to Support Employees

Senior leadership must challenge managers to do more to alleviate stress and exhaustion—and reward them when they do. Currently, neither is happening often enough. For example, while two-thirds of companies have instructed managers to check in with employees about their workload and well-being, these efforts are generally not incorporated in formal evaluations or per-formance reviews. Our research shows women managers are notably more likely to step up this way, but when the work is not formally part of the job description, it can be overlooked.

To effectively address burnout, companies should measure how managers are supporting their direct reports as part of performance reviews. Without accountability and formal recognition, this critical work could be at risk of being relegated to the office housework or work that contributes to the business but doesn't typically lead to advancement or compensation.

Companywide actions are a necessary complement to the work that managers are already doing to address burnout. Burnout is trending the wrong way, but the above actions are key to turning it around.

Women are caught in the ultimate burnout catch-22: They suffer it more and also do more to combat it. Managers are in the best position to spot and address burnout, but senior leadership has a role to play too, by establishing norms, empowering managers, and recognizing their efforts. With this, companies can catch an elusive win-win: creating a better workplace and helping women at the same time.

Adapted from content posted on hbr.org, October 22, 2021 (product #H06N4A).

Take Control of Your Workload

9

How to Get Through an Extremely Busy Time at Work

by Alice Boyes

You're an accountant deep in tax season, a junior doctor in residency, or an entrepreneur juggling a startup and an actual baby. Many of us go through seasons of life when we have very little personal time. Others may be committed to jobs that regularly involve intense and long hours, creating a long-term lack of rest.

While this kind of overwork is not ideal, there are undoubtedly situations in which it becomes a necessity or makes personal sense. I've certainly done it for periods of my life, for instance, in the lead-up to exams or to put final polishes on my books. At times like this, when having a full weekend off seems like a distant dream, advice on the importance of maintaining work-life balance, reducing stress, and getting enough sleep can feel like a slap in the face. You don't need to be scolded to work less. You need practical tips for surviving and thriving when you have to be fully committed. Here are some strategies that can help.

Use Premack's Principle

Premack's principle (as it applies here) is to use an easier behavior as a reward for a harder behavior. For instance, you can reward yourself for finishing a cognitively demanding task (like writing a complex report) by completing a low-key but necessary task, like running an errand that helps you stay organized. This approach can help you pace yourself during your workday, ensuring that you get regular breaks during which your mind can shift into a more relaxed gear while still being productive. Think of it like recovering from bursts of running by walking instead of stopping.

Compartmentalize

Tasks you actually enjoy can become tense, unpleasant experiences if, while you're doing them, you're mentally elsewhere, feeling stressed and anxious about the other hundred things on your list. What's quite pleasurable or satisfying for you, even though it's time consuming? Perhaps it's figuring out how best to present an intricate data visualization. Maybe it's rehearsing speeches in front of friends or family.

If you know the task is important and you're approaching it efficiently, allow yourself to enjoy it. For recurrent hard assignments, think about the parts of it you like best at the beginning, middle, and end stages. For instance, I like listening to my Mac auto-read drafts of my blog posts when doing my final edits. It's satisfying to find those last few instances where I've repeated a word or made a typo, or where the melody of a sentence is wrong. I also like the beginning stages of projects in which I get to top up my brain with broad searches on Google Scholar, and the middle stages when I'm wrestling with parts of what I'm writing that aren't working but when my overall structure is in place and sound. By articulating distinct, enjoyable aspects of tasks, you can be more mindful and savor them.

Save Small Scraps of Time for Mental Rest

When you're very busy, it's tempting to try to cram productive activity, like responding to email or thinking through decisions, into any small crack of time. This could be when you're standing in line at the supermarket, waiting for a presentation to start, or in the five minutes between finishing one thing and joining a meeting. When you're very busy, it can seem essential to work during these moments. However, you don't have to. Instead, consider using brief waiting times for true mental breaks. Take some slow breaths, drop your shoulders, and just chill.

You don't need to take an all-or-nothing approach to this tip, of course. If using small scraps of time to keep work moving sometimes suits you, keep doing it Monday to Friday, but on the weekend, consider giving yourself those little breaks. Find the balance that works for you.

Add Physical Decompression Rituals to Your Day

When we're overloaded, we can hold a lot of physical tension. This is partly due to our in-built fight, flight, freeze response to fear or stress. For instance, the evolutionary basis of clenched fists is your cave-person self preparing to run or punch. Some people breathe faster when they're stressed. Some adopt an aggressive, dominant tone of voice or body language. Since these reactions are often unconscious, you'll need prompts to correct them.

Try using context triggers—deciding which moments in the day you'll use to physically decompress. For instance, maybe you can take some slow breaths whenever you go to the bathroom, just after you wake up, or just before you get into bed. You can also use emotions as triggers, like "When I notice I feel stressed, I'll scan my body for tension and soften and release any spots I find." If you're not sure how to do this, just try opening and closing your fists a few times, clenching and unclenching your jaw, or scrunching and dropping your shoulders. Our thoughts, emotions, and bodily reactions are a feedback loop. When you mimic the physiology of someone who is relaxed, you'll find that your thinking becomes less closed, and psychologically challenging activities in which you need to think openly, like taking in feedback, will seem easier.

Pair Pleasure Experiences with Other Activities

In my book *The Healthy Mind Toolkit*, I wrote about how people often put off pleasure, especially when they feel too busy or undeserving because they haven't gotten enough done. You can buffer yourself against the stress of feeling rushed and overloaded if you repeatedly pair simple sources of pleasure with particular activities you're not as excited to do. For instance, I pack peanut butter sandwiches whenever I fly, which is about the only time I ever eat them, and now the two experiences are mentally linked. No matter how stressed I am about my trip or all the work I need to do before, during, and after it, I feel just a little bit more relaxed because I've packed that treat for myself. Or, if you love podcasts, perhaps you have a routine of listening to specific shows on your commute home each day. If what you love isn't as simple as sandwiches or podcasts, set aside just a bit of consistent time to indulge in your interest, so you've removed decision-making as a barrier. For instance, if cooking is your passion, perhaps you whip up a big batch of something on Sundays that you can then take as lunch for the week.

Just to be clear: I'm not saying that you can life-hack your way through being a permanent workaholic. But when, on balance, overworking makes short- or long-term sense (or is a necessity), you need some harm-minimization strategies. It's important to pace yourself and not let your obligations consume you.

Adapted from content posted on hbr.org, March 26, 2019 (product #H04V4S).

10

Let's Do Less Dead-End Work

A conversation with Lise Vesterlund

Women are expected and asked to do thankless tasks—order lunch, handle less-valued clients—more than men, and research shows that doing those tasks slows down our career advancement and makes us unhappy at work. Why do we wind up with so much office drudgery, and how do we get some of it off our plates?

Women at Work cohosts Amy Bernstein, Sarah Green Carmichael, and Nicole Torres spoke with University of Pittsburgh economics professor Lise Vesterlund about why women get stuck with—even volunteer for—tasks that won't show off our skills or get us promoted, and how that slows down our career advancement and makes us unhappy at work.

LISE VESTERLUND: For a long time, I've been concerned about the fact that women, despite overall improvements in the labor market, still struggle to break through the glass ceiling. Maybe the reason they're not leaning in more is because they're being held back by what we characterize as non-promotable tasks. A non-promotable task could be a client that doesn't bring in a lot of revenue to the firm or where the requirements of the task are quite limited.

NICOLE TORRES: What are the implications of this? If women are volunteering for tasks that won't get them promoted and if they're doing these jobs more than men, how does this hold them back in their careers?

LISE: If you're trying to determine which of two candidates to promote, you're likely to select the one who completed a set of tasks that demonstrated their unique skills. If women more than men have a portfolio of tasks that are less promotable, then they're not going to get promoted as quickly. In fact, they may never get promoted. In terms of advancement, it's not advantageous for women to end up with these tasks. We're finding that in a lot of places, women's happiness at work is limited relative to men's—especially in the field of engineering. In engineering, women report ending up with tasks that are very different from what they thought they were getting trained for. This includes engineers from top schools.

Men and women are going to college, getting their degrees, entering the labor market, and then the women are more likely to report being unsatisfied with the tasks they're given at work. If you're constantly asked to fill in for someone else and are assigned tasks that don't show off your potential, you're not going to be happy at work or perform as well as you could have if you'd had a more challenging and exciting task. It has very serious consequences for women in terms of promotability, but also their overall attachment to a labor market influenced by a portfolio of tasks that are less promotable.

AMY BERNSTEIN: Is it advisable to call out the work as non-promotable?

LISE: That's not advisable because most firms will argue that all work is promotable. It's a question of saying, "Many of my tasks have become routine. Can I get tasks that demand more, where I can show off my skills?"

NICOLE: These tasks change over the course of your career, too. Something can be non-promotable to a higher-ranking senior executive, but it might be promotable to someone more junior.

LISE: Absolutely. If you're a junior partner, taking on a low-profile case and demonstrating that you can do a good job by yourself is very likely a promotable task.

When you become a senior partner, that's probably not a promotable task. Serving on a hiring committee, for example, is extremely important to an organization, and it's probably a good place to start when you're junior in a firm, but later on, serving on a hiring committee is not going to get you noticed. It changes across your career.

AMY: The simple-minded way of dealing with this would be to say, "No, I won't do this anymore." But the world is not usually welcoming to that kind of response. How do you deal with the backlash of saying no?

LISE: We're not recommending that people just start saying no. Part of what I find exciting about this work is that beliefs play such a large role. I've done a lot of work on gender and competition as well. We find that men are more competitive and overconfident. We don't want to tell women, "You should be super-competitive and over-confident," because those are not necessarily the leaders that we really want. In this case, it's easier to figure out what to do, because if it's a question of beliefs, we can move those around. Go back to your firm and say, "Who ends up taking on these tasks every time?" Making it clear that women are not signing up to do the holiday party because there's nothing better to do and really clarifying to the institutions that they are losing out by having these differential task assignments. If I have a group of males and females with MBAs, the best way to run my corporation is to figure out who is the most talented. I'm not going to figure that out if all my female new hires are working on non-promotable tasks. From the firm's perspective, having differences in allocations before even identifying their underlying talent is clearly not optimal. I've spoken to corporations that started coaching women: They tell the women that when they come into a meeting and already know that a project or a client that is less promotable is getting assigned, the women should "look at the body language of your male colleagues as this project comes up and nobody wants to take it." They tell the women to mimic the body language that men have as they start checking their phones, putting things away, or pulling back from the table. Then you don't end up in a position where you suddenly feel so stressed by the silence that you're the one who says yes.

SARAH GREEN CARMICHAEL: What if the manager calls on you and says, "Can you take this on?" Is there a way to say no in the moment without incurring backlash?

LISE: You don't want to be a naysayer. But there are ways that you can negotiate it a little bit. If you're in a public meeting, saying no in front of others isn't advisable. But going up to the manager afterward and saying, "The projects I've been assigned recently are all of the same character. If I'm taking this on, can I not take on the next one? Or can we assign the other non-promotable work to someone else?" When I first got my job, I was assigned to be on the website committee. I responded by saying, "The website committee is a very nice committee, but I would really like to be on the hiring committee instead, where I would actually have some impact."

SARAH: I've been in that position, and I usually say something like, "I'd love to be a good team player and help out with this," or "I'd really like to be in a position where I could help." Then I give the reason why I can't. I try to nod to what's expected of me as a female. "Oh, I would love to be helpful, but unfortunately I can't." Short of asking people in gender-isolated settings to volunteer for tasks at work, is there a way that we can get men to volunteer more, or to say yes more when we ask them to do things?

LISE: A lot of men don't recognize that not stepping up to a task means that a woman is likely to do it. When people volunteer, it's not because they really want to do the task. Or, if you said no to volunteering, it really means that you're putting this additional burden on women.

AMY: You've formed a group to cope with this problem?

LISE: The whole project came out of a "no" club. We were five women, all finding ourselves in the same situation, where the work that we really enjoyed was accounting for a smaller and smaller share. So once a month, we met and talked about the requests that we had gotten, and the things that we had said yes and no to. I would get requests that I felt underqualified for. I would feel like the only time I'd ever be asked is right now, so if I don't say yes now (even if it's going to kill me), they will never ask me again. A very common trigger for women is, "I can get it turned around really quickly and just get it done." I would often be in the position where I would get a request and feel very selfish for saying no. I never considered that the "yes" meant that I was saying no to something else. What the club helped me become aware of was that, by saying, "Yes, I will help you out with that report," I was also saying no to spending time with my deserving kids, who had been waiting all week to see me. Once I became aware of that trade-off, it became easier to say no.

NICOLE: What's an example of something that you brought to the group and the advice they gave you?

LISE: I agreed to be on an editorial board for a very good journal in economics, and I was drowning in editorial work. Initially, they told me, "Don't take the position." But senior mentors advised me that this was very prestigious and that I should say yes. Then I couldn't do it, because it was so much work. I met with the no group on a Friday night over a glass of wine, and they told me that by Monday morning, I needed to resign from the editorial board. The minute I sent the email, I felt like I was hanging out with a bunch of friends who told me to jump off a roof, and I stupidly did it. At the time, I was horrified of the consequences. But it was the only right thing to do. Sometimes saying no is scary. But there's a limit to how many hours you're supposed to be working.

SARAH: Time is the only finite resource that any of us really has. Everything else is fungible, but we all have the same amount of time in a day.

LISE: It's also important to think about the things I really want to say yes to. It's not just saying no, no, no. It's saying no so that you can do the things that you really care about. What is distressing in talking about this is that it's a conversation that you can have with a lot of women. The men appear not to listen so much. It has to be made clear to corporations and business leaders that if they saddle women with more of this non-promotable work, they're not going to find the best talent. It's a corporate responsibility to change the way that we allocate these tasks.

Adapted from "Let's Do Less Dead-End Work," Women at Work *podcast, season 2, episode 1, September 17, 2018.*

11

Learn How to Delegate Effectively

A conversation with Deborah Grayson Riegel and Jasmine LeFlore

D elegating is a leadership skill that benefits you and your team. But determining when and how to delegate which tasks to whom can be overwhelming. And the discomfort many of us feel around assigning responsibilities to others or making requests of our colleagues can lead us to falsely believe it's easier to just continue doing everything ourselves.

To learn how to delegate in a way that delivers the results you're hoping for, Amy Gallo spoke with Jasmine LeFlore, an aerospace engineer who wanted to overcome the awkward, difficult parts of delegating so that she could do more strategic work. She and Amy talked to leadership coach Deborah Grayson Riegel, who shared practices to ensure the work gets done and leaves you and the person you delegated to feeling good about the experience.

AMY GALLO: Jasmine, would you say delegation is something you do a lot already or is it something you want to do a lot more of?

JASMINE LEFLORE: I would say both. For my nonprofit, delegation is important. Right now, I have a cofounder and part-time staff. I've started an apprentice program, where college students who are studying engineering are teaching students about engineering entrepreneurship. My cofounder and I have been following a framework that has been going very well, but as a founder, cofounder, and executive director, I think my time is well suited to working *on* the business instead of *in* the business. Instructing college students to teach this curriculum has been very rewarding. They have fresh eyes and are providing feedback and showing me things that I didn't even think about when I started developing the framework.

AMY: Deb, what do you think about what Jasmine said in terms of the importance of delegation as well as the challenges that many of us face?

DEBORAH GRAYSON RIEGEL: Jasmine hit the nail on the head. As she delegates, she lightens her workload, crosses off her to-do list, and challenges herself, while improving and increasing her value to the organization. There are benefits to the team as well. And she delegates to her peers. We often think about delegating as something we do with direct reports, but Jasmine is delegating to colleagues, which certainly has some benefits. It makes them feel more trusted or respected. They have the opportunity to learn more skills and collaborate more. You might even get a day off if people know how to do what you do. Jasmine is really focused on the benefits not just to herself, but to the team and the organization.

AMY: The idea that delegation isn't just good for you is critically important. Research on delegation by women specifically shows that women tend to delegate less. We also tend to feel more anxiety and guilt about doing so, and that's partly because we see it as a dominant thing to do. Researchers suggest focusing on the benefits of delegating not just for yourself, but for others and how it helps them learn and grow.

DEBORAH: There's research that shows that when women get feedback from all genders, it tends to be about teamwork and collaboration and less about leadership. I want to be mindful that if we are encouraging anyone to delegate more, that we don't just think about it as a teamwork and collaboration skill; we should think about it as a leadership skill as well.

JASMINE: I like feedback and I don't get enough of it. When I do get it, it feels like it's based on collaboration or being organized, but not necessarily the leadership aspects that I'm showcasing.

AMY: Deb, how is delegation a leadership skill?

DEBORAH: To be a leader, you need to be thinking more strategically and less tactically. You need to enable others to grow, develop, and take things on rather than having your hands in every single thing. For you to become a more visionary and strategic coach who guides other people to do the work, you can't be doing everything yourself.

AMY: What steps should we take to decide whether or not to delegate a task, a decision, or a responsibility?

DEBORAH: People have some common misconceptions about what to delegate. They think that they should delegate things that are really boring and small. People should think more broadly about what they can and should be delegating. As you think about your own workload, consider what feels routine for you but may not feel routine for somebody that you're trying to develop. Think about something that is fun for you that you can share with somebody else who might think it's fun. Think about tasks that other people can clearly do better than you can, tasks that eat up your time and that will develop other people so that you can move on to other things. Of course, there are some things that you just shouldn't delegate. One example is if somebody delegated something specifically to you because they wanted you to do it; don't give that to somebody else. Finally, people frequently delegate poorly defined tasks to others when they're not clear of the expectations. They're not clear on the goal, on what success would look like, and they pass that on. As you can imagine, it's a giant game of telephone.

AMY: Jasmine, what tasks are you thinking about delegating?

JASMINE: I'm starting a new project where I'm going to be helping create some virtual interactive demos for our products. I'm coming up with one-page descriptions of what our technology does, the benefits of it, and who it serves. I'm starting with one of our key products but delegating the rest to our younger or early-career engineers is something I'm looking forward to.

AMY: Deb, do you recommend that you either do a piece of the work or do an example of the work before you delegate it? What prep do you need to do before a task is actually ready to pass off?

DEBORAH: You want to think about how they are going to learn what it is you're looking for. Some steps might include being really clear about what you're expecting in terms of the outcome. You might even provide an example of a successful outcome. Distinguish between whether you're looking for a certain outcome or a range of acceptable outcomes. You want to be really clear whether the outcome has to look exactly like this or, once you've agreed on what success looks like, there's a range of possibilities. In addition to providing examples of what it would look like when done well, you want to clarify how the task you're delegating fits into the big picture. A lot of people miss that: putting it in the context of why it matters. Jasmine said she's delegating part of something. How are you going to evaluate progress, process, and outcomes? Those are the things that can really help set up somebody for success.

Adapted from "The Essentials: Delegating Effectively," Women at Work *podcast, season 8, bonus episode, August 25, 2022.*

12

Nine Ways to Say No to Busywork and Unrealistic Deadlines

by Elizabeth Grace Saunders

The difference between living a life of peace and productivity versus a life of stress and resentment could lie in one simple skill: learning how to say no.

Saying no makes the difference between a packed schedule and an open one. It makes the difference between having too many tasks and having just the right amount. It makes the difference between working crazy hours and hitting deadlines without stress.

But saying no can be tough. You might feel uncomfortable saying no because you worry about upsetting people, looking like you can't handle your workload, or missing out on opportunities both now and in the future.

But the truth is that when you never say no, you will actually increase the likelihood of the outcomes you fear. And when you do say no—when necessary—you reduce the likelihood of dropping balls and save your sanity.

So how exactly do you say no? As a time management coach, I regularly coach clients on learning to set boundaries and decline requests when needed. Here are a few of my best strategies for saying no in three critical areas: time commitments, tasks, and time frames.

Time Commitments

To dramatically open up hours in your schedule, you'll need to start saying no to time commitments that aren't the best use of your day. This means diverting yourself from the path of least resistance (accepting all requests that come your way) and instead asking yourself, "Is this the right investment of my time?"

For example, let's say you're asked to volunteer on a committee. It's a good initiative but not aligned with your personal passions or your professional development goals. It would mean at minimum three to five hours out of your work time each month, which add up to 36–60 hours over the course of a year. To decline gracefully say: "Thank you so much for asking me to be part of this committee. I'm really honored, but I'll need to respectfully decline because I'm at capacity right now. Thank you for your understanding."

Or you're asked to attend a meeting where your presence is not necessary. In fact, other people on your team may be a better fit. You might decline the meeting invite and say: "I saw the meeting invite. I appreciate the notice that it's happening. Jerry will be representing our team. I know he'll do a great job and will report back on anything we need to know."

Or perhaps you're invited to go to lunch with individuals who you already see often, and you have a project to work on, want to go to the gym, or simply want a break. You could say: "Thanks so much for the invite, but I already have some other commitments."

Saying no to time commitments that don't align with your priorities or needs can lead to a small amount of initial discomfort but save you hours of time in the end.

Tasks

Most people have far more tasks on their to-do lists than they could possibly get done in a given day. This is especially true for individuals who try to help everyone before getting their own work done. To break out of this cycle, it's time to start saying no.

For instance, when someone asks you to do something that isn't your job, you have every right to say no. But if you've said yes too much in the past, you may need to do some retraining to break people of the habit of asking you for every little thing. They'll learn in time, especially if your response sounds something like one of these:

> *"That's not my area of expertise. I'll give you Cheryl's contact info, and I'm sure she would be happy to help you with that question."*

> *"I think Tim, our intern, can order lunch for tomorrow's meeting. I'll forward the request on to him."*

> *"Typically, the meeting organizer pulls the report for the presentation."*

When you're asked to take on a project that is optional and you already have far more to do than you can get done right now, it's also time to gracefully decline. You could say: "This sounds like a really interesting initiative. Unfortunately, I'm already maxed out on what I can take on right now. I wouldn't be able to get to this for a couple of weeks/months. Since this is important to you, it's probably best to give this to someone who can give it more time and attention."

Finally, when you're in a meeting and people are talking about different tasks that need to get completed but you don't have time to take on more, proceed with caution: Say nothing. Sit on your hands. Don't volunteer. I literally have coaching clients who have me ask them every time we talk: "How many times did you volunteer for things?" Not offering to help is one of the best ways to say no.

Time Frames

Sometimes the tasks that need to get done fall within your responsibility, but it's the timing of requests that causes issues. In these instances, when and where you can, it's helpful to say no to unreasonable schedules.

I know that workplace expectations can vary, so depending on your job, you may not be able to use these strategies. But for those of you who have some latitude, consider these ways to push back on proposed deadlines.

If you get asked to do something small by today when in fact the deadline is somewhat arbitrary, counter with an alternate deadline. Even a day or two of margin can shift something from a frustration that keeps you at the office late to not a big deal: "I would love to help you, but my time is already fully booked with commitments to [my boss, clients, etc.] today. I'll get this back to you by Friday."

This may annoy some people. But hopefully in time, it will teach them to give you more notice. Some departments put in policies for how much lead time they need to turn around documents—for example, two or three days.

If you are often pinged in the evenings and the weekends, and you have the ability to set boundaries, do. Never having downtime can significantly contribute to burnout. One way to avoid unexpected after-hours work is to stay away from your work phone and email. But if you must say something, send a reply like this: "Hi, Joe! I just wanted to let you know that I saw an email from you. I'll review your request first thing when I get back in the office."

Finally, if you receive a large project that you do need to do but the initial deadline isn't reasonable given your other commitments, you can negotiate in a few ways. If the situation involves your boss, you can explain your different priorities and ask for direction on what to focus on first. If the situation involves someone other than your boss but you have the ability to set limits, you can come back to them with a counterproposal. If the situation involves someone other than your boss where you don't have the authority to push back on deadlines, you may need to involve your boss in those conversations. In the end, the phrasing will likely sound something like this: "I hear that you would like this by the end of the month. But with the other projects we have going on, it won't be possible to meet that deadline. I would like to propose a deadline of mid next month. Does that sound reasonable?"

These conversations may also lead to discussions around pulling in other resources, such as contractors, or rebalancing the work.

Saying no isn't easy. But it's worth it. As you consider using these suggested tips and phrases in your own work, make sure you communicate quickly. People can typically take a no more easily when you don't delay.

And communicate with confidence. You don't need to be overly apologetic. Say what you need to say and then move on. Remember, by saying no, you're saying yes to what matters most with your time.

Adapted from "9 Ways to Say No to Busywork and Unrealistic Deadlines," on hbr.org, March 29, 2019 (product #H04V96).

13

How to Say No
After Saying Yes

by Melody Wilding

icture it—a colleague asks if you can chair a new committee they're starting. Without even pausing to think, the first words out of your mouth are, "Sure. I'd love to!" Flash forward, and you're looking at emails piling up in your inbox and a flurry of appointments on your calendar. It suddenly hits you that you're spread too thin. You know you need to say no after having said yes, but you're hesitant to back out of the obligation after you've already given your word.

Saying no is never easy, but it's particularly challenging after you've already said yes to a commitment. You may worry that backing out will burn bridges, cause you to be perceived as flaky or unreliable, or lead to you being labeled a poor team player. These fears are heightened for "sensitive strivers"—highly sensitive high-achievers—who tend to overthink situations and have a hard time setting boundaries.

If you can relate, then the thought of retracting your agreement and facing the brunt of another person's disappointment or anger at you may be too much to bear. This reaction makes sense, since studies show that the brain makes no distinction between possible social rejection and physical pain.[1] Instead, you grit your teeth and follow through with the commitment—sometimes at the expense of your own well-being, which backfires. Not only does it result in excess stress for you, but others may be able to sense that you're distracted, overwhelmed, or resentful.

Whether you have overbooked yourself, realized you have a conflict, or otherwise can't or don't want to participate in a project, it's essential to uncommit gracefully. Doing so will keep your reputation intact and your relationships strong. Here's how to go about saying no with tact and professionalism after you've already said yes.

Consider the Cost

Before you deliver the news, make sure that backing out is in fact the right decision. Consider the opportunity cost. For example, let's say you've said yes to a new initiative from your boss, but now you're having second thoughts about participating. Evaluate how crucial the project is to key business priorities. If the initiative would give you exposure to other parts of the company or allow you to build social capital or new skills, then it may be worth the sacrifice. However, if the costs outweigh the benefits (such as the impact on your personal life or your current projects), then it's better to withdraw.

Shift Your Perspective

If you're paranoid that saying no after you've already said yes will make you appear irresponsible, embrace the fact that it would be selfish and inappropriate to follow through on the task knowing you couldn't complete it. You may feel like you're being generous and helpful by agreeing, but if you can't follow through on your promises, it's not a recipe for high performance, personal happiness, or strong relationships. Plus, consider the positive traits you display when you back out gracefully. You exemplify strong prioritization, time management, and transparent communication—all qualities of powerful leadership.

Be Diplomatic but Truthful

When delivering your message, be assertive and clear without overexplaining. In other words, aim to be direct, thoughtful, and above all else, honest. For example, if you are pulling out of your friend's committee, you might say: "When I said I could join the committee last month, I fully believed I had enough bandwidth to do a great job. After taking a closer look at my calendar, I realized I've overextended myself and there are several professional commitments I can't move. This means I won't be able to participate as chair."

Providing a short explanation or justification for your reasoning can help your withdrawal be better received. For instance, you could explain, "I know we talked about me joining as committee chair, but when I agreed I didn't expect a big project would be assigned to me at work. Because of that, I need to decline." In the case of backing out of the initiative with your boss, you could share, "I've had the chance to review my priorities and this new project would stop me from contributing to my core job responsibilities at the highest level. That wouldn't be the right—or best—decision for myself or the team, so I have to respectfully change my yes to a no."

Preserve the Relationship

It's appropriate to apologize and take responsibility for any mistake, misunderstanding, or simply overextending yourself. After all, the other person was counting on you and may have been making plans around your participation. In the case of withdrawing from the committee, you could say, "I'm sorry for any inconvenience this causes. It means a lot that you thought of me for this opportunity and I'm rooting for it to be a success. I can't wait to hear how everything goes." Expressing gratitude and ending on a positive tone shows care and compassion.

Offer an Alternative

Propose a different timeline or reschedule to a new date if you genuinely want to help. Take a raincheck and leave the door open to say yes in the future by saying, "After revisiting my schedule, I need to change my decision and decline this invitation right now. But please keep me in mind for the future. Would you reach out again in a few months?"

You can also avoid leaving the person in a lurch by suggesting an alternative. Perhaps you offer to introduce the person to a coworker who can help or a contractor they could hire. Maybe you redirect the person to a resource that can help them such as a community, podcast, or training material that can meet their needs or solve their problem.

Learn from It

Backing out of commitments isn't fun or comfortable, but it can provide a valuable lesson and an impetus to overcome people-pleasing tendencies that may be standing in your way of being more successful. Use this as a learning opportunity to build greater discernment around what you do—or don't—agree to in the future. Going forward, try to say yes only to opportunities that excite you and ones you have room for.

No matter how thoughtful you are, you may need to occasionally go back on a promise you've made or change your mind. Don't make it a habit but do approach the situation with sensitivity and consideration to get the best possible outcome.

Adapted from content posted on hbr.org, September 20, 2021 (product #H06L6E).

14

All the Help We Can Get

A conversation with Heidi Grant

Asking for help isn't easy, especially when everyone around you is also maxed out. We assume that our request will be an imposition, or we worry that it'll make us look like we can't handle our jobs. Fortunately, the research shows that these fears are largely unfounded.

Social psychologist Heidi Grant spoke with Amy Gallo about asking for help while conveying confidence and strengthening your relationships with colleagues. She explained how to ask in a way that can improve your chances of getting a yes and why lending a hand to others is good for you too.

AMY GALLO: What makes it more likely that someone will actually say yes to a request for help?

HEIDI GRANT: First and foremost, people are more likely to say yes than we realize. There are great studies on this.

Vanessa Bohns, a professor at Cornell, researched this along with her colleagues. If you wanted to put a number on it, we are about twice as likely to help as we think we'll be. In other words, if I ask somebody for help, they're about twice as likely to say yes than I think. We're already wildly underestimating the odds that other people will say yes, but there are some things you could do to make it a little bit more likely that someone will say yes to you. There are some common mistakes we make when it comes to asking for help. One of the most important things to focus on is the medium in which we ask for help. Typically, we ask for help by sending someone an email or a text. The reason we do that is because it's more comfortable for us as the askers to not have that conversation live. I can send you an email or a text message and hope for the best because they're not live interactions. Unfortunately, that's the worst thing you can do. Live interactions are vastly more likely to lead to someone saying yes. In one of Vanessa's studies, people were 30 times more likely to say yes if they were asked during a live, in-person conversation to help, rather than via an email.

AMY: Is that because it's easy to send a text or email saying no?

HEIDI: Exactly. The reason we want to ask for help in a way that feels more comfortable for us is the exact reason we get more nos. It feels more comfortable for them to say no to us. Pick up a phone or get on a video call. You'll be more likely to get a yes. People always say, "I have to do it over email. This is the nature of work. We communicate this way." The other mistake we make is sending group emails. We'll email 20 people, hoping that one of them will help us with something. The problem is, they see that there are 19 other people on the email thread, which leads to what psychologists call "diffusion of responsibility." People think, "This isn't being directed at me specifically. It's being directed at all of us. One of the other people is probably going to say yes, so I don't have to do this." You don't want to make somebody feel like they're just one in a crowd that is being asked for help. Make any request for help feel personal, either because it's a live conversation or because you're addressing only that person. Explain why their help is specifically the help you need. Those things dramatically increase the chances someone will say yes.

AMY: The requests that I'm happy to help with are the ones where the person's been really clear about why I'm the one they asked. It makes me feel useful, effective, even special.

HEIDI: That's exactly the right way to think about it. It increases the chances you're going to get a yes. It also increases the quality of the help you're given. People will say yes much more often than we think they will. But they won't necessarily give you their best help. Very often we give people a minimum amount of help to either get it off our plate, absolve us from guilt, or not damage the relationship. Making it clear why a certain person is uniquely able to help you increases the chances you're going to get maximum help. They're going to help you in ways you didn't even consider because it boosts their self-esteem. It's both about getting a yes, but also about getting a really good yes.

AMY: I would almost rather get a no to my request than a half-hearted yes.

HEIDI: When people can imagine the impact that their help will have on you, they're more likely to give the best help they can. We ask for help, but we don't explain how it will be helpful and then we fail to follow up. If you ask someone to do something of significance for you, you need to follow up with them to let them know the impact that it had, because that's the moment they're going to feel like it was rewarding, and it keeps them coming back. They'll be a resource you can tap into again and again because this person knows that every time they help you, they feel great about it.

AMY: Many of us feel some obstacles when we're asking for help. One of the biggest for me is knowing what I need help with. I know I'm drowning, I'm overwhelmed, and I'm not going to be able to do all this, but I don't even know what to ask for. Do you have any advice on figuring that out?

HEIDI: You have to take a little bit of time to reflect. Look at your to-do list, identify some of the things that are stressing you out the most, and pause to ask yourself where you could use help. Are there components that someone could help you with? Block a half hour on your calendar each week to say, "OK, what's on my plate for this week and what can I ask for help with?" Potential sources of help will surface. Part of what can make us feel like we don't have support is that we operate under an illusion of transparency. We feel like our needs, thoughts, and feelings are obvious to other people because they're obvious to us. But nothing could be further from the truth. Even those who see you every day don't know that you need help. We also forget how dangerous it is to offer unsolicited help. When I offer unsolicited help to my daughter, the look I get reads, "Mom, I can do it myself. I don't need your help." People can get offended by offers of help, and it sometimes keeps other people from offering us help. If they don't know we want it, they don't want to risk offending us by offering it. So, you really do have to articulate your needs, and then you will find that there are lots of people in your life who will help. You need to take the first step.

Adapted from "All the Help We Can Get," Women at Work podcast, season 6, episode 1, October 5, 2020.

Carve Out Time for Yourself

15

To Reduce the Strain of Overwork, Learn to Listen to Your Body

by Stephanie J. Creary and Karen Locke

I f there was one constant theme in Bianca's life, it was constantly pushing herself to meet others' expectations. She became an accountant because her grandfather told her that it was a good job. At work, Bianca (not her real name) also pushed herself to meet others' ideals. "They paid me well enough to be able to get blood from a stone. I let my company suck me into that hole." Years of working toward others' ideals eventually took a toll on Bianca's mental and physical health. "Management was ruthless," she shared. "It got to a point where there was no work-life balance, I was coming home, working all night, yelling at my kids. . . . The stress just seeped into my family life. I ended up having anxiety issues. My health went downhill."

Bianca's story of overwork may feel uncomfortably familiar. Decades of research shows that workplaces are often grounded in "ideal worker" norms that reward employees for always being ready, willing, and able to work.[1] To cope with these demands, some workers internalize them and live according to the "work hard, play hard" mantra—that is, they valorize overwork in both work and nonwork settings as a means of striving for balance, pushing themselves in both realms. Others maintain a willingness to commit to overwork during the week, so long as they can use the weekend as an attempt to recuperate. Yet, by Monday, both groups become caught up once again in the same work grind. Over time, adhering to ideal worker norms can result in breakdowns of the body and mind.

Our research explores a unique way workers can navigate the ideal worker image and break this vicious cycle of overwork and recuperation: through experiencing a community outside of work that taps into bodily awareness.[2] Specifically, we examine how people experience, use, and express their bodies when engaging in various work and nonwork tasks—something called "somatic engagement." We do this by drawing on two year-long studies of yoga teacher training.

Most importantly, we find that people can learn to adjust overwork patterns in and outside work by learning to engage differently with their bodies. By growing to understand what somatic strain felt like during yoga teacher training, participants were able to understand how and when similar feelings occurred in other areas of their lives. And when they started to recognize these sensations on the job, it led them to question their own overwork patterns and resist them. In short, they began to view their bodies from a place of self-acceptance rather than as an instrument for maximizing performance.

We gained these insights through ethnographic research methods. Specifically, we each enrolled and participated in different yoga teacher programs to answer our research questions. Stephanie had prior experience teaching and practicing yoga and was interested in studying how different types of relationships shape professional identity development. Karen also had prior experience practicing yoga and was interested in the implications of mind-body practices for the workplace. As required by our universities' institutional review boards, we disclosed our dual roles as researcher and participant in the first formal session of our respective training programs. Common to ethnographic research, we participated in all activities that were expected of trainees.

What Participants Learned in Yoga Teacher Training

Prior to joining yoga teacher training, people in our study largely accepted overworking as a given and took their bodies for granted, treating them as instruments to support work performance. When they faltered, participants perceived these experiences as a letdown or inconvenience relative to work demands.

Many initially saw yoga teacher training as an opportunity to restore their bodies. One participant said, "I went into [the teacher training] thinking, 'OK, I'll stretch my body and I'll feel better.'" Another signed up for the training because she had been taking yoga classes after work as a means to unwind and "always felt good afterward." A different participant decided to join when her marriage was facing difficulty because she "needed to take some physical and mental space for herself."

Over the course of our research, participants (including Bianca) learned to alter how they engaged their bodies in different activities and settings. They also began to call into question their operating ideals regarding overwork, to think of it as a problem consistent with Western cultures, and to understand overwork as a point of differentiation from yogic beliefs. One participant noted, "In the West, we're never taught to say you can't. . . . My mom would kill me. We have to do it all, soccer mom, mother, friend." This feeling transferred over into yoga, too, resulting in the need to "push, push, push" through challenge and intensity to perform an arm balance or some complex, twisted shape.

Over time, trainees learned how to scan their bodies, to become aware of their bodily experience of overwork as they held a challenging yoga pose, and to identify where their body felt like it was tense and straining. They learned to notice when and where they felt themselves gripping and consider possibilities for softening. Further, formal assignments and encouragement from senior trainers directed trainees to "take off the mat" what they were learning in the yoga program. As a result, sharing personal stories of recognizing and adjusting to overwork tendencies were normal and expected as part of trainees supporting each other's development. Weekly philosophy sessions often began with a check-in on participants' work and personal lives in which trainees shared and discussed key moments, including their own overworking behaviors.

Ultimately, participants recognized their yoga communities as a source of encouragement and support that had helped them to identify and respond to their patterns of overworking, whether that meant encouraging each other to let go when struggling with learning Sanskrit terms, when memorizing yoga sequences became overwhelming, or when competitive dynamics at work became stressful.

The Work-Yoga Connection

Importantly, our research showed that the ability to monitor and adjust their somatic engagement to stop overwork

in yoga teacher training was generalizable to our participants' lives more broadly. They now could catch themselves, pause, and pull back from overwork by lessening
reactivity, reducing their time working, and reducing
physical and mental straining. A schoolteacher who
developed awareness of her habit of feeling "I've got to
finish, I've got to finish" noted that she could now recognize that feeling in her body and mind and "consciously
undo it." "Yes, a project needed to be completed," she
noted "but did it need to be finished *now*?"

A chief financial officer came to recognize that she
would become very tight when she became unhelpfully
impatient with her direct reports; when that happened,
she learned to pause and breathe. A health counselor
noted that she had become able to be less reactive
when dealing with frustrations at work; she could now
catch herself and "be more discerning and make more
of a choice about" her response and following actions.
Broadly, connecting action and awareness enabled participants to pause, engage with how they were feeling,
and make more reflective adjustments to their overworking behavior patterns.

In addition, we found that by the end of yoga teacher
training, participants began to question the value of
being an ideal worker in the first place. They no longer
needed to be the "type A personality," the "control freak,"
the one who could do it all—at all times. Instead, they
saw themselves as the kind of person who prioritizes their

own needs. For instance, in the past, a teacher took pride in the fact that she never took time off from work regardless of how she was feeling, going 20 years without taking a sick day. After yoga teacher training, she found herself working to be the kind of person who honored her body and took personal time when she felt she needed it.

Participants felt like they could still be a teacher, a lawyer, or an accountant—but they could be an accountant who *also* sees themselves as a practicing yogi who attends to and adjusts their patterns of overworking. This can have positive implications for more than just the yogis. For example, a development manager was able to pull back from constantly driving her team; as she did, she found it was easier for her direct reports to make their own contributions.

Finally, our study revealed that continuing membership in the yoga community beyond the teacher training programs solidified it as a kind of "third place"—that is, a place beyond work and home that helped participants resist overwork, broaden themselves, and lead richer lives. After the training ended, participants met for coffee, had football game watch parties during the week, shared information about unique opportunities to practice together (such as sunset classes on paddleboards), and even invited each other to special work events.

For Bianca, continued engagement in the community also enriched her family life. "[The yoga community] nourishes me and helps me manage the family. I even said to my kids, 'Do you like mommy on yoga or without yoga?' And they're like, 'On yoga! On yoga!' . . . So that's why I keep going."

We studied yoga teacher training, but our research can also apply to people who regularly participate in fitness, athletic, or other somatic practice communities. But use caution; some communities may reinforce the forms of somatic engagement underlying overwork. Activities such as running marathons, CrossFit, or even power yoga may be less effective in moderating overwork norms because they reinforce the very same competitive and perfectionist ideals underlying many workplace cultures.

As people become more aware of the downsides of ideal worker norms, there's no shortage of tips on how to think about and manage overwork. Ours is a bit different, but no less effective: Seek out communities beyond work and home that counter the trends of excessive striving and all-encompassing work schedules, and that bring awareness to your body. This can feel daunting; you must be intentional about wanting to develop more sustainable ways of being. But our research suggests that it can be a challenge worth accepting.

Adapted from content posted on hbr.org, November 16, 2021 (product #H06OZ5).

16

How We Take Care of Ourselves

A conversation with Ashley Whillans

I t can be a challenge to take care of ourselves when we're on deadline, traveling too much, or reporting to a boss who emails at all hours. Hosts Amy Bernstein and Nicole Torres spoke with researcher Ashley Whillans, who revealed how managers can model healthy habits and how employees can make time to practice them. She also highlighted the importance of spending time doing things that give us meaning, purpose, and a sense of belonging.

ASHLEY WHILLANS: I'm a subjective well-being researcher; I study happiness. When I think about self-care, I think about the predictors of happiness. Do I have enough time to spend with people that I care about? What is the quality of my social interactions? Am I on my phone the whole time? Am I rushing from point A to point B, meeting

A and meeting B, spa appointment one to lunch date two, so that I'm not actually deriving any satisfaction from my social interactions? Do I have meaningful work that feels purposeful? What are the kinds of things I'm doing at work? Do I feel like I have control over my time, my schedule, the tasks that I'm completing? Do I feel optimistic about where my life is going? When I think about self-care, I think about the outcome of self-care, which is well-being and meaning in life. Then I work backward from there to think about the predictors of well-being.

NICOLE TORRES: That's a helpful view of self-care as a holistic journey that also includes work and interactions with people. It's not just a marketing concept; it's not just face masks and massages. Self-care is a lot bigger than that. That's helpful as I think about how self-care fits into my life. I've always thought of work and self-care as being separate. Isn't prioritizing my career and spending a lot of time at work and trying to advance taking care of my future self?

ASHLEY: We all have multiple goals, needs, and motivations in life. I think about the structure of our whole days and how we're spending our time. Does it map onto the things that we care about? The more that the way we spend each day aligns with all of these things that you're talking about—having a productive and fulfilling career, feeling like you're moving forward in it, having productive social relationships, having me time—those all fit within buckets or categories of things that you care about, your values, and your goals. The extent to which you spend your days in a way that's consistent or aligned with these goals, values, and aspirations creates this feeling of self-care and everything being coherent. Then your work isn't necessarily in conflict with your personal life; it's part of a greater whole. It's one motivation fulfilled in one area. Having a diverse set of motivations will make you happier and healthier as a whole person.

AMY BERNSTEIN: I've learned that I need to figure out what helps me function happily. If it means going to the gym and cutting into the nine-to-five workday, that's OK. That's what I need and it's the only time I can do it. It means I'm going to be healthier, my head is going to be on straight, and I'll be able to function better. As a manager I need to communicate this, particularly to women in the office, because it gives them permission to take care of themselves as well.

ASHLEY: That's where managers need to start communicating, especially to groups—junior people, women—and having very clear guidelines for how you ask for personal time in the workplace. In some of the data that I've collected on asking for more time on adjustable deadlines at work, employees who do it and feel like they can are, unsurprisingly, less burned out, are happier, and perform better because they asked for more time and turned in higher-quality work. The problem is that junior people and women, who could benefit most from additional time, are the ones who are least likely to ask for it because they think they're going to be penalized, even though my data doesn't show different penalties based on gender or on junior-senior status. If I take that time off, if I'm the person who's going to go to the gym in the middle of my workday, I still have a sneaking suspicion that a promotion might go to the person in the corner office who's working all the time. We know what to do to get self-care, but how does it operate in practice?

AMY: The other thing to consider is the notion of the ideal employee. Some of it is just resetting our expectations and articulating goals that are more human for everyone, starting with the corner office.

ASHLEY: There's research showing that if managers truly disconnect on their vacation, then employees are more likely to do that too.

AMY: It's why you don't send emails after a certain hour or on the weekends.

ASHLEY: In American work culture, to get employees to take these kinds of benefits and truly disconnect, data suggests you have to regulate people taking time off if they're not going to spontaneously do it. They still have an idea in their minds of the ideal employee. We need to set a cultural norm that it's not OK to constantly check Slack and email; that's not the ideal employee. The ideal employee works really hard when they're in the office and then goes home at a reasonable time and has a self-care-filled life outside the office. When you have a whole self that's not just work, you perform better.

AMY: I had imagined that self-care was about massages and going to the gym and making sure that you make time for you. What I now understand is that it's doing what you need to do to feel whole. That includes maintaining your personal relationships and taking care of *who* matters to you in addition to what matters to you.

ASHLEY: It's about spending the minutes, moments, hours, and days of your life in a way that's consistent with the things and people you care about. Sometimes taking care of our kids and people we care about feels stressful in the moment. But they're exactly the kinds of things that give us meaning, purpose, and a sense of belonging.

Adapted from "How We Take Care of Ourselves," Women at Work *podcast, season 4, episode 5, November 11, 2019.*

17

How to Take Better Breaks at Work, According to Research

by Zhanna Lyubykh and Duygu Biricik Gulseren

For many of us, being productive means spending more time working. It seems intuitive that the more time we spend on job tasks, the more we can get done. And not surprisingly, the popular literature is rife with advice on how to maximize work time. For example, the daily routines of CEOs often include things like waking up at 4 a.m., working on the weekend, and even being strategic about how often they go to the bathroom. To tackle an ever-increasing workload, many workers choose to grind through, skip lunch, and stay after hours.

But the cost of being always on (and doing it well) is high. More than half of employees (59%) report feeling burnout, according to a recent survey from Aflac.[1]

Engagement has taken the opposite turn and is declining among U.S. workers. Alarmingly, both high burnout and low engagement rates are associated with hindered performance. What can we do to address our declining well-being while maintaining performance?

Pausing work rather than pushing through might help with both aspects. Intrigued by two competing narratives—one focused on working more as an indicator of performance and the other on having regular respites to protect well-being—as well as mixed (and sometimes even conflicting) findings of individual studies on these topics, our team conducted a systematic review of existing research on workplace breaks.[2] In analyzing more than 80 studies, we (with our colleagues Zahra Premji, Timothy Wingate, Connie Deng, Lisa Bélanger, and Nick Turner) confirmed that pausing work throughout the day can improve well-being and also help with getting more work done. Counter to the popular narrative of working long hours, our research suggests that taking breaks within work hours not only does not detract from performance but can help boost it.

Why Is Taking Breaks Beneficial for Well-Being and Performance?

Like batteries that need to be recharged, we all have a limited pool of physical and psychological resources.

When our batteries run low, we feel depleted, exhausted, and stressed out.

Pushing through work when very little energy is left in the tank puts a strain on well-being and work performance. In extreme cases, nonstop work can lead to a negative spiral: A worker tries to finish tasks despite their depleted state and is unable to do them well and even makes mistakes, resulting in more work and even fewer resources left to tackle those same tasks. This means that the more we work, the less productive and more exhausted we can become. Think about reading the same line for the fifth time, for example, and still not absorbing it.

The good news is that taking breaks can help employees to recharge and short-circuit the negative spiral of exhaustion and decreasing productivity. However, not all breaks are equal in terms of their effects.

What Types of Breaks Are More Effective for Improving Well-Being and Performance?

Breaks come in many different shapes and forms: exercising, browsing social media, going for a short walk, socializing with others, taking a nap, grabbing lunch, and so on. However, our systematic review shows that not all break types are equally effective. In other words, it matters *how* to pause work. The following are some common break elements to consider.

Break length and timing

A longer break does not necessarily equate to a better break. Disengaging from work only for a few minutes but on a regular basis (micro-breaks) can be sufficient for preventing exhaustion and boosting performance. For example, workers can take short breaks for snacking, stretching, or simply gazing out the window. Further, timing of the break matters—shorter breaks are more effective in the morning, while longer breaks are more beneficial in the late afternoon. This is because fatigue worsens over the workday, and we need more break time in the afternoon to recharge.

Location of breaks

Where breaks take place can make a big difference in terms of recovery. Both stretching at a desk and going outside for a short walk seem like very similar break activities, but they might substantially differ in their recharging potential. Our review demonstrates that taking a break outdoors and enjoying green space is far better for recharging workers' resources than simply staying at a desk.

Break activity

Engaging in physical activity during a break is effective for improving both well-being and performance. Exercising is an especially valuable recovery tool for mentally demanding work. However, the positive effects of this break type are short-lived, and employees need to exercise regularly to yield its benefits.

Despite these benefits, exercise is not the most preferred way to spend breaks among employees. Our review shows that browsing social media is the most common break type—almost everyone (97%) reports engaging in this activity. However, researchers find that scrolling through social media during work breaks can lead to emotional exhaustion.[3] As a result, people end up with diminished creativity and work engagement instead of replenished resources. As such, this type of break may not be effective for boosting performance.

Furry break companions

One study in our review showed that interactions with a dog can lower levels of cortisol hormone, an objective indicator of stress.[4] More research is needed in this area, as the effects on performance remain unclear. We do, however, have a strong suspicion that spending a break with a furry companion is effective for many employees.

Research shows that interactions with pets can substantially boost individuals' psychological well-being, which in turn is strongly linked to performance.[5]

What Can Managers and Organizations Do to Encourage Breaks?

The mere availability of breaks does not guarantee benefits. Workers may not use their breaks in the most efficient ways or take them at all. As decision-makers and role models in organizations, managers are in an important position to encourage effective work breaks. This can be achieved in several ways.

Foster positive attitudes toward breaks

While employees are generally positive about breaks and report that they are beneficial for performance, managers do not always share this sentiment. This can deter people from recharging. Thus, it is critical that managers are informed about the performance-related benefits of work breaks. For example, HR managers can incorporate this information in the company's wellness training programs. Organizations can also consider implementing wellness moments (akin to safety moments) during which they can share their strategies for taking effective breaks and brainstorm fun break activities. Even hanging posters about the benefits of and best practices in taking breaks in the workplace can go a long way.

Take breaks themselves

Managers can communicate the importance of taking breaks by taking the most effective types regularly, which employees can mimic. For example, a manager who regularly walks her dog in a nearby park can communicate to her employees that she'll be stepping away from work for a bit to do so. Such a strategy not only sets a positive example, but also sets clear boundaries around not interrupting breaks. Leading by example will help prevent the possible stigma and guilt associated with taking breaks. It's promising that more and more organizational leaders are recognizing this and even share their regrets about not taking sufficient time off work.

Schedule dedicated break times

Our review shows that many employees are unable to take regular breaks or are dissuaded from doing so because of the stigma; thus, we recommend that managers and organizations schedule dedicated break times. Such break times need to be implemented with care. Rigid break schedules, such as mandating that employees stop working only at a certain time and of a predetermined length, reduce employees' autonomy and can even have harmful effects on them. We recommend offering break periods of a certain length such as one hour a day and leaving when and how often they want to take their breaks at the employee's discretion. Offering flexible work schedules, innovative workplace break initiatives such as break tickets (for example, giving daily tickets that allow employees to take off an hour of their choice), or providing on-site social or physical activities could be some examples of optimal break scheduling.

Create spaces for breaks

As we have highlighted, the location of breaks can play an important role in maximizing their benefits. For example, a small park or indoor green space can communicate the organization's commitment to facilitating work breaks and enhance the benefits of breaks in relation to employee performance. To further yield the benefits of outdoor breaks, you could also have an off-leash dog park where employees who enjoy interacting with animals can do so. This can also serve as a recruitment tool, as the demand for pet-friendly workplaces is rising, and many companies have already adopted pet-friendly policies.

Organizations with employees working from home can also use the spaces available to them by arranging online park meetings where remote workers can join the meeting while walking or sitting at a convenient outdoor space. Alternatively, they can allocate a break budget for employees to create their own break space. For example, employees can buy an indoor plant or a yoga mat.

Employee performance has always been a concern for organizations, and more are making efforts to address employee well-being. Work breaks are a promising tool to improve both. Organizations need to recognize the importance of breaks and engage in deliberate efforts to facilitate their effectiveness.

Adapted from content posted on hbr.org, May 31, 2023 (product #H07NKF).

18

How Organizations Can Support Women's Mental Health at Work

by Kelly Greenwood

While men and women have similar rates of mental health conditions overall, women face specific challenges around mental health in the workplace. Some are tied to gender roles and stereotypes, and some are intersectional in nature. Mental health is intersectional, since identity markers such as race and gender shape an individual's experience; it's also an emerging diversity, equity, and inclusion (DEI) category in and of itself.

The list of challenges affecting women is long. For one, women are more prone to certain diagnoses. They are twice as likely as men to experience depression, generalized anxiety disorder, and PTSD, and much more likely to battle eating disorders. Pay inequity, caregiving responsibilities, and gender-based violence are among the contributing risk factors to common mental health conditions. Infertility, menopause, and postpartum depression also affect many. Physical and emotional caregiving roles—as daughters, mothers, colleagues, and even leaders—result in heavier burdens. Then there's being underrepresented in leadership at work, navigating double-only status as a woman of color or member of the LGBTQ+ community, enduring sexual harassment, dealing with imposter syndrome, juggling parental leave, and having office housekeeping roles. Many of these challenges are largely invisible, since women may be reluctant to discuss them at all, much less at work.

Add these up, and it's no surprise that gender adds another layer of complexity to workplace mental health. The structures and systems of most companies were built with men in mind. Many women may not be inclined to "other" themselves further by disclosing a mental health challenge.

Between my gender and generalized anxiety disorder, I've had a lot to navigate, and I've done my fair share of covering. This has been the case in environments ranging from male-dominated management consulting at the start of my career to my current role as founder and former CEO of Mind Share Partners, a nonprofit driving culture change on workplace mental health.

Here's what to do if you're a woman struggling with your mental health at work, or if you're a leader who wants to create a mentally healthy environment for your female employees. Many of these recommendations are standard to supporting mental health at work, but the nuances and context of being a woman make applying them much more difficult.

How Can Women Advocate for Their Own Mental Health at Work?

Despite the systemic issues at play, there are practical ways that you can advocate for your mental health in the workplace. These include identifying and asking for what you need, finding allies and safe spaces, talking to your manager or HR, and evaluating your culture to decide whether it supports you in the ways you want.

Reflect on your needs

First, think through the nature of your mental health and your specific challenge. Is it chronic, episodic, or a one-time event? Consider the contributing factors. Are they work-related or limited to your personal life? Is there a gender-specific component, like childcare or workplace discrimination, that might make you more reluctant to discuss the problem at work? Be clear about the effects. Is your mental health challenge affecting your work performance?

Talk with a friend, family member, or therapist about your concerns and brainstorm the potential asks that you could make at work to support yourself. You may also want to get advice from a women's circle or ask female friends to recommend therapists, books, or podcasts that focus on gender. Consider whether seeking out the mental health benefits and other resources your employer provides (such as health-care coverage to see a therapist or psychiatrist) is sufficient or if you need an accommodation (such as starting your workday later). It may help to educate you about the legal protections available to you.

Find allies and safe spaces

The first person at work I ever disclosed my generalized anxiety disorder to was a female mentor who had previously opened up about a family member's mental health struggles. Without this knowledge, I wouldn't have had the courage to seek her guidance when I was underperforming as a direct result of my anxiety.

Given the stigma often associated with mental health challenges, finding a safe space to tell your story and receive support from allies is a critical step. Simply realizing that you're not alone can go a long way, especially when you may be feeling othered because of your gender. This can happen one-on-one or through your company's women's affinity group or mental health employee resource group. Peer support is a powerful lever to reduce stigma.

Allies can help you see that mental health challenges can be useful for developing workplace strengths. Combined with the added difficulty of navigating gender at work, allies can teach us empathy and resilience, spur creativity, and fuel our ambition.

If there aren't any obvious mental health allies at your company (of any gender), look for potential indicators. Has someone expressed vulnerability or talked authentically about personal challenges of any kind? Has a male leader referenced his working wife or daughter in a supportive way? Test the waters to see how they respond to, say, a celebrity who's been in the news for talking about her mental health or an upcoming fundraising walk in your community to support a mental health organization. Then consider seeking their advice on how to navigate your specific workplace.

Talk to your manager or HR

If you need accommodations for your mental health or have suggestions that could benefit everyone, talk with your manager (or HR if you don't feel comfortable with your manager). This can be scary. Mind Share Partners' 2021 Mental Health at Work Report found that women respondents were less comfortable talking about their mental health to managers and HR than men were, but no difference existed when talking to colleagues or friends.[1] Power dynamics are at play, sometimes made more pronounced by gender. You may fear putting an already hard-to-come-by promotion in jeopardy or othering yourself with a mental health challenge or stereotypically female concern such as childcare or eldercare.

You control how much you choose to share and with whom. Your ask can be as simple as, "Could I take Friday off? I've been feeling a little burned out lately." You might mention your diagnosis, if you have a close, trusting relationship. If your proposed solution involves changes to workplace factors that could benefit everyone on your team, such as increased flexibility or norms around afterhours response times, you might introduce the idea of a work-style conversation with your manager. This sets up everyone to do their best work and supports mental health without having to name it. Should you require a separate accommodation, you'll likely have to say a bit more and ideally work with your manager and HR to co-create a solution.

Even in a female-led workplace, my own self-stigma and fear of professional repercussions were so strong that, as a new hire trying to prove myself, I didn't ask for the simple accommodation to see my therapist in-person weekly. Had I done that early on, I would have saved my manager, organization, and myself a lot of hardship. Reflect on the trade-offs of sharing; they may increasingly be weighted toward disclosure as mental health challenges become more normalized, especially among high performers.

Evaluate the culture

While quitting is a last resort when your job is hurting your mental health, it should always be on the table. Before you make that decision, take a step back and consider your company's culture. Are there women in leadership? Is there anyone who has openly talked about their mental health or other challenges? Is the executive team open to feedback and change? Is it committed to DEI and new ways of working that promote balance and well-being?

You shouldn't have to jeopardize your mental health to earn a living. Fortunately, companies are realizing that more and more as employee priorities around mental health play out through recruitment and retention. It's OK to walk away from work that isn't working. The 2021 Mental Health at Work Report found that 68% of millennials and 81% of Gen Zers have left jobs for mental health reasons, compared with 50% of respondents overall. The report also found that women are less likely than men to positively view their organization's culture around mental health. A study from Deloitte showed that women who work for gender-inclusive organizations have higher levels of mental well-being and loyalty to their employers.[2] To compete for talent, companies will have to make changes, as younger generations are increasingly prioritizing their mental health and the work cultures that support it.

How Can Leaders Support Women's Mental Health?

Unless we're in positions of power, there is only so much that individual women can do to advocate for our mental health. Leaders, managers, and HR must drive culture change to correct for historically male-dominated workplaces. To do just that, we offer the following advice, much of it adapted with women in mind from the Mind Share Partners' Ecosystem of a Mentally Healthy Workplace framework.[3]

Provide mental health training and over-communicate resources

Leaders must prioritize mental health training for people at all levels, including executive teams, managers, and individual contributors. Due to generational and other differences in the workplace, everyone should have the same level of understanding, including how mental health intersects with the various aspects of our identities—gender and otherwise.

Take a proactive, preventive approach with a management lens. It isn't necessary to dive into signs and symptoms. Mental health training should provide baseline knowledge, discuss intersectionality, dispel myths, and offer tools and strategies to navigate workplace mental health, such as how to have difficult conversations and create mentally healthy cultures.

In addition, leaders should regularly communicate about the mental health benefits available. These should be embedded in companywide emails at least monthly and be prominently featured on the intranet, instead of buried deep within a benefits portal. Since many people delay seeking treatment due to stigma, leaders should ideally also share if they have personally used the benefits, to normalize doing so. This should also be true of other benefits that women may not want to discuss openly, such as those for infertility.

Build mental health into policies, practices, and measurement

Name mental health explicitly in relevant policies and incorporate it into organizationwide practices. Examples include paid time off and leaves as well as flexible hours and healthy communication norms. Companies should establish a genuine commitment to DEI, including having executive sponsors and funding for employee resource groups.

In addition, leaders must rectify structural issues that harm women, such as pay inequity, insufficient parental leaves, and lack of consequences for microaggressions and harassment. Leaders can incite positive changes through accountability mechanisms such as regular pulse surveys. Measuring female employee engagement, retention, and dimensions of mental health cements the support of women's mental health as an organizational priority.

Foster inclusive flexibility and sustainable ways of working

Workplace factors such as lack of autonomy, unrealistic workloads, and lack of boundaries after hours can lead to poor mental health. For women, these can be even more detrimental due to microaggressions, caregiving responsibilities, and other factors. I often avoided mentioning my two small children to external male stakeholders for fear of biases about my capacity to simultaneously be a mother and a driven entrepreneur.

Leaders should build as much flexibility as possible into policies and practices. Every woman and every individual will need something different, be it remote work or flexible hours. Be sure to revisit this with your direct reports since shifts happen over time and with life changes, such as parenthood.

Leaders should model sustainable and flexible work practices themselves. Otherwise, female employees are unlikely to change their behavior, for fear of negative implications for their careers. Even in the most support-ive environments, we typically have to unlearn a lifetime of conditioning—be it workaholism or mental health stigma. Many women learn to put their own needs last, to be people pleasers rather than to speak up for themselves, and to do the extra emotional labor required to balance being strong and nurturing leaders. This can make pri-oritizing mental health at work exceedingly difficult. We should give ourselves grace and remember that we can only be effective once we've first taken care of ourselves, including our mental health.

Be the change

Authentic leadership is an extremely effective, evidence-based way to gain trust and lessen stigma. Being vulner-able and sharing about your own mental health or other challenges is one of the most powerful things you can do. It signals to employees that they can discuss what was once taboo in the workplace and helps them feel com-fortable sharing.

While it was a long time coming, as CEO of Mind-Share Partners, I freely talked about my past mental health challenges and pushed myself to share my strug-gles in real time to benefit my team. These ranged from debilitating depression that led to a leave of absence, to grief about my dad's unexpected passing immediately before the Covid-19 pandemic, to hot flashes due to peri-menopause, which felt particularly off-limits, given my early days in male-dominated consulting. Revealing that last one ended up being an unexpected win since my team gifted me a mini desk fan that plugged into my laptop! Members of my team told me how refreshing it was to see a female leader be vulnerable. As a result of my sharing, they could openly discuss their own mental health and personal challenges for the first time ever at work, which allowed us to offer support and adjust as needed.

Modeling mentally healthy behaviors and building a culture of connection are also essential, especially for women, who may be hesitant to disrupt the status quo. Just telling people that it's OK to take a vacation or log off after working hours does nothing if you don't follow that same advice. For example, I put my therapy appointments and events for my kids' school on my work calendar. My team knew that they could also prioritize important personal things during the workday and that kids could pop into our video meetings. Checking in regularly on a personal level with each of your direct reports fosters a caring and inclusive culture. This can be as simple as reserving the first five minutes of a meeting to genuinely ask, "How are you, and how can I help?"

. . .

Reorienting to supporting women's mental health at work will ultimately benefit everyone, from dads who want to be more involved parents to Gen Zers who expect flexibility by default. Hopefully there will come a time when we won't have to separate out the needs of women, but instead will have achieved true culture change and inclusion.

Adapted from content posted on hbr.org, March 18, 2022 (product #H06X31).

NOTES

Chapter 1

1. Irene Padavic, Robin J. Ely, and Erin M. Reid, "Explaining the Persistence of Gender Inequality: The Work-Family Narrative as a Social Defense Against the 24/7 Work Culture," *Administrative Science Quarterly* 65, no. 1 (2019): 61–111.

Chapter 2

1. "The Great Renegotiation: New Report Rings Alarm That Nearly Half of Women Executives in Revenue Roles Are Considering Leaving Their Company," Women in Revenue, June 13, 2022, https:// womeninrevenue.org/resources/the-great-renegotiation-new-report -rings-alarm-that-nearly-half-of-women-executives-in-revenue-roles -are-considering-leaving-their-company/.

2. Kelly Shue, "Women Aren't Promoted Because Managers Underestimate Their Potential," *Yale Insights*, September 17, 2021, https://insights.som.yale.edu/insights/women-arent-promoted -because-managers-underestimate-their-potential.

3. Lila MacLellan, "70% of Top Male Earners in the US Have a Spouse Who Stays Home," Yahoo! Finance, April 30, 2019, https:// finance.yahoo.com/news/70-top-male-earners-us-162154561.html.

Notes

Chapter 3

1. Emerging Technology from the arXiv, "Your Brain Limits You to Just Five BFFs," *MIT Technology Review*, April 29, 2016, https://www .technology review.com/2016/04/29/160438/your-brain-limits-you-to -just-five-bffs/.

Chapter 6

1. Elizabeth Kolbert, "Why Facts Don't Change Our Minds," *New Yorker*, February 27, 2017.

2. Howard J. Klein et al., "When Goals Are Known: The Effects of Audience Relative Status on Goal Commitment and Performance," *Journal of Applied Psychology* 105, no. 4 (2020): 372–389.

Chapter 7

1. "Burn-out an 'Occupational Phenomenon': International Classification of Diseases," World Health Organization, May 28, 2019, https://www.who.int/news/item/28-05-2019-burn-out-an -occupational-phenomenon-international-classification-of-diseases.

2. Christina Maslach and Michael P. Leiter, "Understanding the Burnout Experience: Recent Research and Its Implications for Psychiatry," *World Psychiatry* 15, no. 2 (2016): 103–111, https://www .ncbi.nlm.nih.gov/pmc/articles/PMC4911781/.

3. Nancy Beauregard et al., "Gendered Pathways to Burnout: Results from the SALVEO Study," *Annals of Work Exposures and Health* 62, no. 4 (2018): 426–437, https://www.ncbi.nlm.nih.gov/pmc /articles/PMC5905644/.

4. Maslach and Leiter, "Understanding the Burnout Experience."

5. "Paid Time Off Trends in the U.S.," U.S. Travel Association, n.d., https://www.ustravel.org/sites/default/files/media_root /document/Paid%20Time%20Off%20Trends%20Fact%20Sheet.pdf.

6. Robin J. Ely and Irene Padavic, "What's Really Holding Women Back," *Harvard Business Review*, March–April 2020.

Chapter 8

1. "Debunking Four Myths That Hold Women Back," *Women in the Workplace 2023*, McKinsey & Company, https://womenintheworkplace.com/.

Chapter 13

1. Elitsa Dermendzhiyska, "Rejection Kills," Aeon, April 30, 2019, https://aeon.co/essays/health-warning-social-rejection-doesnt-only-hurt-it-kills.

Chapter 15

1. Tracy L. Dumas and Jeffrey Sanchez-Burks, "The Professional, the Personal, and the Ideal Worker: Pressures and Objectives Shaping the Boundary Between Life Domains," *Academy of Management Annals* 9, no. 1 (2015): 803–843.

2. Stephanie J. Creary and Karen Locke, "Breaking the Cycle of Overwork and Recuperation: Altering Somatic Engagement Across Boundaries," *Organization Science* 33, no. 3 (2021): 873–1249.

Chapter 17

1. "Employee Well-Being and Mental Health, Workplace Benefits Trends, 2022–2023," Aflac Work Forces Report, https://www.aflac.com/docs/awr/pdf/2022-trends-and-topics/2022-aflac-awr-employee-well-being-and-mental-health.pdf.

2. Zhanna Lyubykh et al., "Role of Work Breaks in Well-Being and Performance: A Systematic Review and Research Agenda," *Journal of Occupational Health Psychology* 27, no. 5 (2022): 470–487.

3. Hongjai Rhee and Sudong Kim, "Effects of Breaks on Regaining Vitality at Work: An Empirical Comparison of 'Conventional' and 'Smart Phone' Breaks," *Computers in Human Behavior* 57 (2016): 160–167.

4. Kristyna Machova et al., "Canine-Assisted Therapy Improves Well-Being in Nurses," *International Journal of Environmental Research and Public Health* 16, no. 19 (2019).

5. M. Wells and R. Perrine, "Critters in the Cube Farm: Perceived Psychological and Organizational Effects of Pets in the Workplace," *Journal of Occupational Health Psychology* 6, no. 1 (2001): 81–87.

Chapter 18

1. "2021 Mental Health at Work Report," Mind Share Partners, https://www.mindsharepartners.org/mentalhealthatworkreport-2021.

2. "Women @ Work 2023: A Global Outlook," Deloitte, https://www.deloitte.com/global/en/issues/work/content/women-at-work-global-outlook.html.

3. "Key Frameworks for Success: Creating Mentally Healthy Workplaces & Programs," Mind Share Partners, https://www.mindsharepartners.org/developingaworkplacementalhealthstrategy.

INDEX

Discussion Guide

Since the *Women at Work* podcast first launched, we've heard from people worldwide that it has inspired discussions and listening groups. We hope that this book does the same—that you'll want to share what you've learned with others. The questions in this discussion guide will help you talk about the challenges women face in the workplace and how we can work together to overcome them.

You don't need to have read the book from start to finish to participate. To get the most out of your discussion, think about the size of your group. A big group has the advantage of spreading ideas more widely—whether throughout your organization or among your friends and peers—but might lose some of the honesty and connection a small group would have. You may want to assign someone to lead the discussion to ensure that all participants are included, especially if some attendees are joining virtually. And it's a good idea to establish ground rules around privacy and confidentiality. *Women at Work* topics touch on difficult issues surrounding sexism and racism, so consider using trigger warnings.

Finally, think about what you want to accomplish in your discussion. Do you want to create a network of mutual support? Hope to disrupt the status quo? Or are you simply looking for an empathetic ear? With your goals in mind, use the questions that follow to advance the conversation about women at work.

1. Overwork is one symptom of a destructive workplace environment that can result in cognitive overload, mental and physical exhaustion, and burnout. Across your organization, do you feel that a culture of overwork is normalized? Do long work hours feel necessary to advance? Do you notice a difference between the ways in which the women versus the men conduct their work?

2. In chapter 1, the authors make the argument that women aren't held back due to the challenge of balancing the demands of work and family, but that the problem lies in a cycle of overwork and burnout. Is this something you agree with, and have you experienced it firsthand? What can be done to stop the cycle?

3. Chapter 2 reveals five maladaptations that women make to adapt to the business cultures around them, including: I need to be perfect, I need to fit in to rise, I need to sacrifice to succeed, I need to do it alone, and success means having it all. Have you fallen victim to any of these maladaptations? What happened and how did it affect your well-being? What can women do to evolve beyond these maladaptations to reclaim a sense of agency?

4. To what degree has your job influenced your identity? If your identity has become enmeshed with your career, what can you do to build a more balanced one that aligns with your values?

5. Mandy O'Neill believes that cognitive load creates problems with distraction. Do you find yourself struggling to focus because you have a second shift outside work, take on too many tasks, or are generally burned out? How can practicing compassion for yourself help to offset some of your cognitive load and burnout?

6. Burnout is a serious issue. How can you recognize the signs of burnout and what can be done to overcome it? What can companies do to better address the needs of burned-out workers across all genders?

7. In chapter 9, Alice Boyes states that there will be times throughout your career when overworking (short or long term) is required. What harm-minimization strategies can you take during times when it's necessary to overwork?

8. According to Lise Vesterlund, women often get stuck with non-promotable tasks. Can you think of an instance when you were assigned or even volunteered for a task that you knew wouldn't show off your skills or help you to advance? How can you delicately turn down a dead-end task in the future?

9. Consider your current to-do list. When and how might you delegate some of the tasks on this list? Is delegation something you already do, or is it something you'd like to do more of in the future?

10. Do you feel comfortable saying no to a request, or do you worry about upsetting people, looking like you can't handle your workload, or missing out on opportunities? If you find yourself struggling to turn down a task, what tips can you employ from chapter 12 to make the process more comfortable?

11. If someone approached you for help, what could they say that would make you more likely to lend a hand? Conversely, if you approach someone for help, how would you phrase the ask and the follow-up?

12. In what ways have you tapped into a community outside work for emotional support, body awareness, or stress relief? Has it made a noticeable difference in your well-being when you're back at the office?

13. What healthy habits do you model at work? What healthy habits does your manager model? Do you find that these habits translate into helping direct reports practice a healthier work-life balance?

14. How can women advocate for their own mental health at work? What can companies do to support the mental health of their female employees?

ABOUT THE CONTRIBUTORS

Amy Bernstein, *Women at Work* cohost, is the editor of *Harvard Business Review,* where she oversees the magazine and its team of editors. She's also the vice president and executive editorial director for Harvard Business Publishing, responsible for the editorial strategy and content development of the learning and educator assets for HBP's Corporate Learning and Higher Education businesses.

Sarah Green Carmichael, former *Women at Work* cohost, is an editor and columnist at Bloomberg. She is a former executive editor at *Harvard Business Review.*

Amy Gallo, *Women at Work* cohost, is a contributing editor at *Harvard Business Review* and the author of two books: *Getting Along: How to Work with Anyone (Even Difficult People)* and the *HBR Guide to Dealing with Conflict.* She writes and speaks about workplace dynamics.

Watch her TEDx Talk on conflict, and follow her on LinkedIn.

Nicole Torres, former *Women at Work* cohost, is a managing editor at Bloomberg. She is a former senior editor at *Harvard Business Review.*

Alice Boyes is a former clinical psychologist turned writer and the author of *The Healthy Mind Toolkit, The Anxiety Toolkit,* and *Stress-Free Productivity.*

Tiffany Burns is a partner in McKinsey's Atlanta office. She serves consumer and retail clients on organizational transformations that significantly improve performance. Tiffany leads McKinsey's retail store practice in North America as well as McKinsey's efforts to support racial equity for Black Americans, or 10 Actions. She also oversees the firm's internal initiatives and external partnerships with nonprofits and organizations committed to driving change in their local communities.

Ellen Keithline Byrne is a cofounder of Her New Standard: The Playbook for Women Leaders, a leadership consulting firm focusing on advancing women in leadership, which designs boot camps for women leaders on the rise. Find Ellen and her partners discussing strategies for women leaders on LinkedIn and Instagram.

Stephanie J. Creary is an assistant professor of management and an organizational behavior scholar at the Wharton School of the University of Pennsylvania. Her research examines how people manage multiple identities, boundaries, and inclusion in organizations while navigating any tensions associated with doing so.

Robin J. Ely is the Diane Doerge Wilson Professor of Business Administration at Harvard Business School and the faculty chair of the HBS Race, Gender & Equity Initiative.

Heidi Grant is a social psychologist who researches, writes, and speaks about the science of leadership and motivation. She's the associate director of the Motivation Science Center at Columbia Business School and the director of research and development in learning at EY.

Kelly Greenwood is the founder and former CEO of Mind Share Partners, a national nonprofit changing the culture of workplace mental health so that both employees and organizations can thrive. Through movement building, custom training, and strategic advising, it normalizes mental health challenges and promotes sustainable ways of working to create a mentally healthy workforce.

Duygu Biricik Gulseren is an assistant professor at the School of Human Resources Management at York University, Toronto, Canada, and chair of the Canadian

Society for Industrial and Organizational Psychology. Her research focuses on healthy work and leadership.

Jess Huang is a partner in McKinsey's Bay Area office. She leads McKinsey's Commerce Media work and partners with consumer-facing clients to boost company growth and drive commercial effectiveness. As an expert in research and customer analytics, Jess brings expertise in data and insights to her work to advance women and other diverse groups in business, including pathways to greater parity for women in retail and media, as well as greater inclusion for LGBTQ+ employees, Asian Americans, and other people of color.

Lisa Kaplowitz is the executive director of the Rutgers Center for Women in Business and an associate professor of professional practice in the finance department at Rutgers Business School. She has 25 years of experience as an investment banker and CFO and routinely speaks on issues related to gender equity and advancing women in business. Her TEDx Talk, "Advancing Women by Redistributing the Housework, One Son at a Time," highlights the need for equal distribution of household responsibilities.

Janna Koretz is a psychologist and the founder of Azimuth, which provides therapy focused on career enmeshment, values work, and burnout.

Alexis Krivkovich is the managing partner for McKinsey's Bay Area office and oversees fintech efforts in North America. She serves financial services and technology companies as they seek to align their organizations for growth and productivity. Alexis is passionate about supporting executive teams to execute on their diversity strategies and invests deeply in sponsoring younger women to build thriving careers.

Jasmine LeFlore is an aerospace engineer at Raytheon Technologies and runs Greater Than Tech, a nonprofit that teaches girls about engineering and business.

Karen Locke is the Pat and Margaret Walsh Professor of Leadership and Ethics at William & Mary's Raymond A. Mason School of Business. Her current research focuses on embodiment's participation in stability and change, and her methodological scholarship examines data analysis and writing practices in qualitative research. She is the recipient of the Research Methods Division's 2019 Distinguished Career Award at the Academy of Management.

Zhanna Lyubykh is an assistant professor of management and organization studies at the Beedie School of Business, Simon Fraser University, Vancouver, Canada. Her research focuses on employee well-being, workplace mistreatment, and leadership.

Kate Northrup supports ambitious people in lighting up the world without burning themselves out. She's the bestselling author of *Money: A Love Story* and *Do Less*, the creator of the *Do Less Planner*, and the host of the podcast *Plenty*.

Mandy O'Neill is an associate professor of management at the George Mason University School of Business and a senior scientist at the university's Center for the Advancement of Well-Being.

Irene Padavic is the Mildred and Claude Pepper Distinguished Professor of Sociology, Emerita, Florida State University.

Deepa Purushothaman is an executive fellow at Harvard Business School and the founder of the re.write. She is also the author of *The First, The Few, The Only: How Women of Color Can Redefine Power in Corporate America*.

Ishanaa Rambachan is a partner in McKinsey's Bay Area office. She helps major financial institutions across sectors improve their performance, manage risk, and enhance organizational effectiveness. She speaks regularly on risk, financial, and diversity topics. Her passion for building women's leadership capabilities predates her time at the firm; previously, Ishanaa was a Rhodes Scholar at Oxford University, where she focused her research on women's development.

Deborah Grayson Riegel is a communication and presentation skills coach. She is the coauthor of *Overcoming Overthinking* and *Go to Help.*

Elizabeth Grace Saunders is a time management coach and the founder of Real Life E Time Coaching & Speaking. She is the author of *How to Invest Your Time Like Money* and *Divine Time Management.* Find out more at RealLifeE.com.

Lisen Stromberg is an award-winning author, global keynote speaker, and instructor at Stanford University on modern leadership. She is the cofounder of Prism-Work, a leadership and culture transformation consultancy. Her latest bestselling book, *Intentional Power: The 6 Essential Leadership Skills for Triple Bottom Line Impact* provides leaders at every level with the insights they need to move from success to significance in today's complex work environment.

Tijana Trkulja is an engagement manager in McKinsey's New York office. She serves financial institutions on topics of risk and resilience. Tijana has spent significant time researching issues of gender equality, including women in financial services as well as dual-career couples. She is passionate about developing solutions that enable success for women in corporate America and empowering the financial independence of women everywhere.

Lise Vesterlund is the Andrew W. Mellon Professor of Economics at the University of Pittsburgh. She is also a research associate with the National Bureau of Economic Research.

Ashley Whillans is an assistant professor at Harvard Business School and the author of *Time Smart: How to Reclaim Your Time and Live a Happier Life.*

Melody Wilding is an executive coach and the author of *Trust Yourself: Stop Overthinking and Channel Your Emotions for Success at Work.*

Lareina Yee is a senior partner in McKinsey's Bay Area office. She is the chair of the McKinsey Global Technology Council and leads the Tech Innovators Practice. Lareina served as McKinsey's first chief diversity and inclusion officer and is a leading expert on advancing diversity in business, globally championing best practices that companies can use to build diversity into the core of their success strategy.

Women *at* Work
Inspiring conversations, advancing together

ABOUT THE PODCAST

Women face gender discrimination throughout our careers. It doesn't have to derail our ambitions, but how do we prepare to deal with it? There's no workplace orientation session about narrowing the wage gap, standing up to interrupting male colleagues, or taking on many other issues we encounter at work. So HBR staffers Amy Bernstein and Amy Gallo are untangling some of the knottiest problems. They interview experts on gender, tell stories about their own experiences, and give lots of practical advice to help you succeed in spite of the obstacles.

Listen and subscribe:
Apple Podcasts, Google Podcasts, Spotify, RSS

Inspiring conversations, advancing together

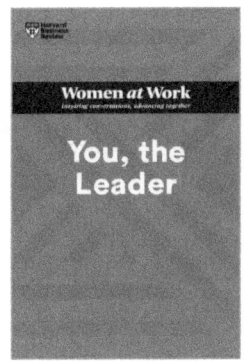

Based on the HBR podcast of the same name, **HBR's Women at Work series** spotlights the real challenges and opportunities women face throughout their careers—and provides inspiration and advice on today's most important workplace topics.